DATE DUE

FOLLETT

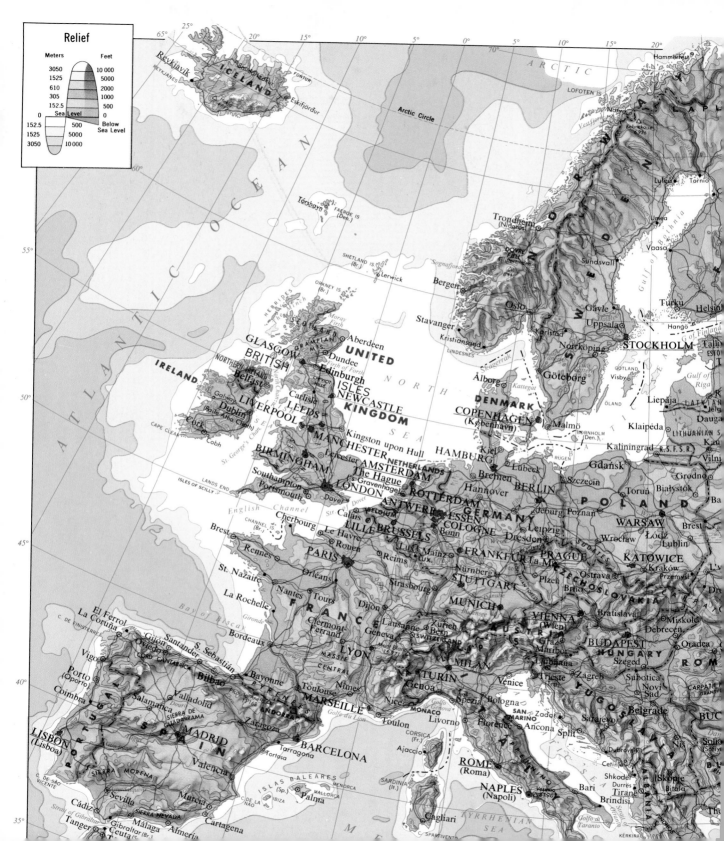

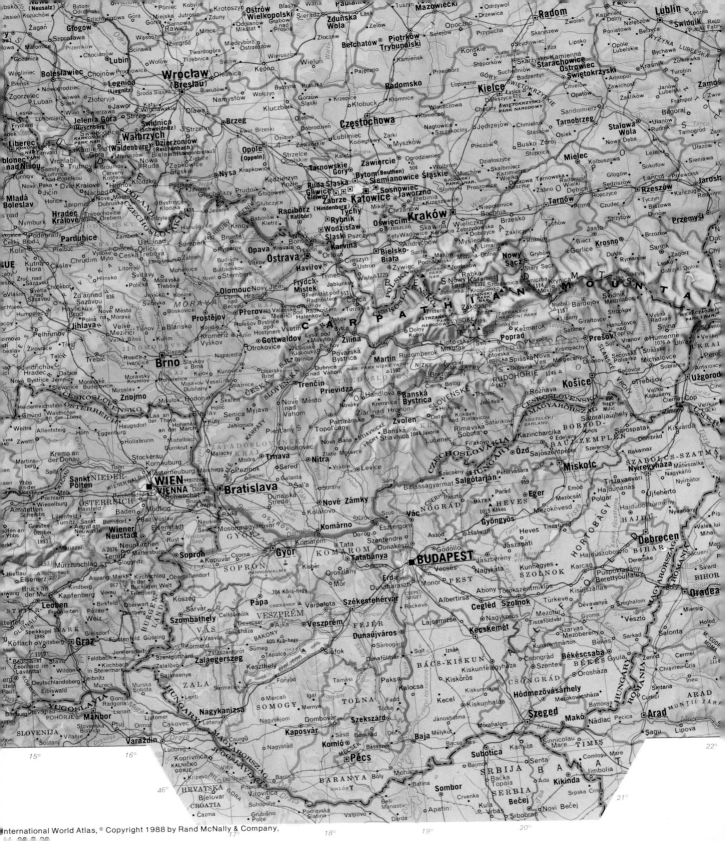

Enchantment of the World

HUNGARY

By Martin Hintz

Consultant: Lawrence W. Lerner, Ph.D., Assistant Director, Russian and East European Studies, The Henry M. Jackson School of International Studies, University of Washington, Seattle, Washington

Consultant for Reading: Robert L. Hillerich, Ph.D., Bowling Green State University, Bowling Green, Ohio

CHILDRENS PRESS ®

CHICAGO

Baroque buildings in Gyor and shop fronts in Szentendre

To my son Stephen

Library of Congress Cataloging-in-Publication Data

Hintz, Martin.
  Hungary / by Martin Hintz ; consultant, Lawrence W.
Lerner ; consultant for reading, Robert L. Hillerich.
      p.   cm. — (Enchantment of the world)
  Includes index.
  Summary: Discusses the geography, history, economics,
and culture of Hungary, an eastern European nation.
  ISBN 0-516-02707-7
  1. Hungary—Juvenile
literature. [1. Hungary.] I. Title. II. Series.
DB906.H48 1988   88-10899
943.9—dc19   CIP
                                            AC

Childrens Press®, Chicago
Copyright © 1988, 1992 by Regensteiner
    Publishing Enterprises, Inc.
All rights reserved. Published simultaneously in Canada.
Printed in the United States of America.

5 6 7 8 9 10 11 12 13 14 R 02 01 00 99 98 97 96

Picture Acknowledgments

Root Resources: © Patricia Preston: 4 (2 photos), 61 (top); © Bill Gleasner: 5, 107 (right), 109 (right), 112 (top); © J.N. Hagar: 17 (left), 18 (left); © Wendel A. Witkay: 18 (right), 68 (bottom), 79; © Kramarz: cover, 19 (left), 48 (right), 54 (top), 66, 69 (left), 73, 83 (left), 84 (left), 98; © Connie Coning: 26, 54 (bottom right); © Thomas R. Schultz: 57 (right), 72; © Irene E. Hubbell: 59 (right); © Dianne Carter: 63 (bottom), 107 (left); © Vera Bradshaw: 67, 85 (right), 93
©**Shostal Associates:** 6 (2 photos), 8 (2 photos), 12, 17 (right), 19 (right), 21 (right), 56 (left), 60 (left), 63 (top left), 83 (right), 88, 108, 112 (bottom)
©**Cameramann International, Ltd.:** 9, 11 (right), 20 (left), 21 (left), 22, 53 (left), 54 (bottom left), 56 (right), 57 (left), 58 (2 photos), 60 (right), 61 (bottom), 62 (3 photos), 69 (right), 70, 74, 76 (right), 78, 85 (left), 86 (2 photos), 95, 97, 103, 111, 113 (far right)
©**Martin Hintz:** 10 (2 photos), 11 (left), 15, 20 (right), 48 (left), 59 (left), 65, 68 (top left and right), 71 (2 photos), 76 (left), 82 (left), 109 (top), 113 (left & center)
Historical Pictures Services, Chicago: 24, 25 (2 photos), 29, 33 (2 photos), 35 (2 photos), 36, 39 (2 photos), 47 (right)
AP/Wide World Photos Inc.: 41, 43, 47 (left), 49, 50, 51 (2 photos), 88 (inset)
© **Bill Hibbard:** 53 (right), 82 (right), 84 (right), 100 (top), 109 (bottom left)
Third Coast Stock Source: © Buck Miller: 63 (top right), 106; © Martin Hintz: 100 (bottom)
Len W. Meents: Maps on 13, 55, 64, 67, 70
Courtesy Flag Research Center, Winchester, Massachusetts 01890: Flag on back cover
Cover: Budapest and the Danube River

Moonrise over the Danube River at Budapest

TABLE OF CONTENTS

Above: Herding horses on the puszta
Below: A shepherd with his flock near Kapuvar

Chapter 1

THE BLEND OF HUNGARY

"Down there, in the sea-flat regions of the Great Plain
That's where I come from, that is my world;
My eagle's soul is liberated from its prison,
When I see the infinity of the plains."

Sandor Petofi (1823-1849)

This vision of Hungary's poet laureate Petofi becomes real in the Kiskunsag National Park near Bugac. Here, on the immense, rolling *puszta*, or plains, of south-central Hungary, a visitor feels the same uplifting spirit of nature described by the young writer more than 130 years ago. Appearances don't change much on the puszta. The same compact, thatched farmhouses dapple the plains. Magnificent herds of brown and black horses thunder across the landscape. A shepherd astride a donkey still scurries after his flock of curly-horned racka sheep.

This is the backwater of the Tisza River area between the cities of Lakitelek and Tiszaalpar. Sand dunes, spotted with rocky ledges, lay sprinkled across the far reaches of the puszta. In the spring, before the raw winds can whip the sand into eye-stinging

Hungarian "cowboys"

lashes, these meadows are sprinkled with brilliantly colored wildflowers. A rainbow of red, white, and yellow petals dances over the pastures as far as the eye can see.

Although this portion of the Hungarian plain is not as table flat as other areas to the east, the expanse of sky and earth is still overpowering. This is the infinity of which Petofi writes.

The horsemen, the "cowboys" of the puszta, have always been a part of Hungary, lending their roughriding image of freedom to the national mystique of what it is to be Hungarian.

The poet's spare words capture the best essence of his homeland. Soaring spirit, love of life, eagerness to discover newness—these are all tied up in the beauty of the green-blue grasses of the plain. The puszta is the Hungarian dreamland, where everything is open and untamed. Even the residents of the country's bustling cities experience the unshackled vibrancy

Farm machinery baling and loading hay

symbolized by that union of sky and landscape. City dwellers love escaping the rush of traffic to vacation on the plains. For their holidays, they appreciate the sweet scent of new-mown hay, the sound of pounding horse hooves, and the sips of fiery *futyulos*, an apricot brandy made on the puszta. The drink is powerful enough to rival the crackle of lightning.

Hungary, however, is certainly more than a rural enclave. There is another Hungary, one that is a truly modern European nation. This Hungary is a blend of heavy industry, a delightfully varied cultural life, and a curious mix of political and economic structures that in the past tied it to both the Western and the Eastern power blocs.

This nation is typified by Budapest, the capital city. Its more than two million inhabitants comprise almost 20 percent of the country's population. On Gellert Hill, high above the Danube River, is the brooding shadow of the massive Soviet war memorial. From this vantage point can be seen the calm, faded

*A view from Gellert Hill (left) and the
Soviet war memorial (right) on the hill*

neighborhoods of Buda and Obuda (Old Buda), ringed by
mountains and filled with gentle gingerbread buildings and
marble statuary. On the opposite side of the mud-brown river is
upstart Pest (pronounced *pesht*), the "young" city of the plains,
with its blocklike new hotels and modern office buildings.

Of course, "young" is a relative term in Hungary. Buda, Obuda,
and Pest have been here for hundreds of years, long before they
were linked under one municipal government in 1870. At first,
due to its flatland location and propensity for being burned to the
ground by invaders, Pest remained a struggling village. Compared
to the seat of Hungarian power situated in regal Buda, Pest was a
backwater. By the time of the union, however, Pest had become
the cultural center of the country. It was discovered by
businessmen, developers, and industrialists who favored the
opportunities presented by level land and the chance to get out
from under the thumb of their neighbors. Pest soon outstripped
the opposite bank in population.

Left: Szechenyi Bridge   Right: Chain Bridge (rear) and Elizabeth Bridge

The three communities retain their reverence for the old ways and a fierce neighborhood pride. Symbols of new Budapest are the six bridges that now physically and philosophically link both banks. They range from the graceful modern span of the Elizabeth Bridge to the more traditional stones of the fabled Szechenyi Bridge. Ferry boats are considered the seventh bridge.

Budapest is Hungary and it is not Hungary, its residents agree, just as the puszta is and is not all that the country is about. This seems confusing, but it really isn't. Both urban and rural areas have their own traditions and dignified outlook on life. The same sturdy, free-spirited people unite the capital, as the symbol of an up-to-date nation, with the open reaches of a more traditional countryside.

There is a mixture of images and life-styles that don't faze the Hungarians. They have a thousand-year tradition of learning, adapting, and growing from each national experience. They have been conquerors and conquered. When that happens, people learn a lot about themselves. The blend is what makes Hungary such an enchanting land.

The Danube near Baja

Chapter 2

A VARIED LAND

The country of Hungary envelopes 35,919 square miles (93,030 square kilometers), about the size of the state of Indiana or the countries of Portugal and Jordan. The greatest distance from east to west is 312 miles (502 kilometers) and, from north to south, 193 miles (311 kilometers). However, even this area is only a mere third of how vast Hungary once was.

Under various Hungarian rulers, the country once extended as far as the Adriatic Seacoast. It also covered most of Romania and Bulgaria, as well as parts of Poland. In 1918, after the horrors of World War I, Hungary lost these extensive territories. Fifty percent of Hungary's population became citizens of new countries carved out of the old empire.

THE DANUBE RIVER

Hungary today is bordered on the north by Slovakia. The northeast neighbor is the new republic of Ukraine and on the east is Romania. Austria lies on the west and the new nation of Slovenia and Yugoslavia on the south.

The mighty green-brown waters of the Danube River run along the northern border with Slovakia. Near the city of Esztergom, the river makes a great bend south to flow through

Budapest and across the Great Plains before crossing the border.

This river is Hungary's major waterway, flowing 255 miles (408 kilometers) within its borders. The Danube is the prime link with trading partners from the North Sea to the Black Sea in the south. Traffic is heavy on the Danube as sleek white excursion boats ply the entire length of the river, passing tubby barges and rusty freighters. An international commission oversees traffic on the river. It makes sure that the waterway is kept clear of obstructions.

THE GREAT PLAINS

At first look, the Great Plains is horizon-to-horizon farmland and cattles ranches. But there are major cities, such as Szeged, a center for processing agricultural goods. The Great Plains makes up the soul of Hungary, stretching across 20,000 square miles (51,780 square kilometers). Scientifically, the Great Plains is called the Great Afold, and covers more than one-half of Hungary's land mass, edging into Romania and Yugoslavia. The dunes and scrub grasses, fertilized fields, and low-lying hills roll on to the south and east like an ocean swell.

Near Debrecen in the far eastern portion of the country is the National Park of Hungary, encompassing 200,000 acres (809,372 hectares). Most of the land is pasture for horses and long-horned gray cattle, carefully bred descendants of the original animals brought to Hungary by the first nomadic invaders from the east.

Hungary ran out of luck several centuries ago when the Turks stormed into the country with torches and *scimitars*, swords with sharp, curved blades. The Turks destroyed most of the towns and

Long-horned cattle on the puszta

cities on the plains, few of which were rebuilt. The word puszta in fact means "barren place."

Nature subsequently reclaimed the once neat farm fields, turning much of the landscape into mosquito-infested swamps. It took many years before anyone wanted to live on the plains again, much of which had to be drained before it could be refarmed. However, the region is again the breadbasket of Hungary.

THE KISALFOLD

In addition to the Great Plains, another flatland lies in the northwest corner bordered by the Danube and Drava rivers. The Kisalfold (Little Plain) covers about a third of Hungary and lies between the Alps and Transdanubian hills. The Danube bisects the fertile soil of this agricultural district. The region abounds with historic towns such as Gyor and Tatabanya.

THE NORTHERN HIGHLANDS

Dense forests carpet the Northern Highlands, but there are open slopes for skiing. The Highlands range along the border with Slovakia from the Danube to the northeast corner of Hungary along the Bodrog River.

The Highland mountains are the remains of ancient volcanic formations comprising the Carpathian range. Mount Istallosko, in the Highland's Bukk (Birch) Mountains, is one of the highest points in Hungary at 3,145 feet (959 meters). Eger, with a minaret dating back to the days of Turkish occupation, and Tokaj, whose Tokay wines are world renowned, are two of the principal cities in the Highlands.

TRANSDANUBIA

Shallow valleys and low hills make up Transdanubia. Three of the nation's largest lakes are found here. Although Lake Balaton is generally calm, fierce summer storms can whip the surface into a lather of foam and spray. Balaton's tepid, shallow waters cover 230 square miles (596 square kilometers). Numerous health resorts, spas, and holiday homes ring its sandy shoreline. Vineyards, producing grapes for Hungary's finest wines, thrive around the lake, which is fed by pure spring waters.

Dozens of bird species live in the swampy region at the western edge of Balaton, where it joins the sluggish, meandering Zala River. They find the reedy water perfect hideaways for their nests.

A quiet square in Eger (left) and a beach at Lake Balaton (right)

WATER DISTRIBUTION

Rainfall in Hungary varies. Only a few inches (thirty millimeters) of rain falls each year on the Great Plains where there are often drought conditions. Upwards of a foot (thirty centimeters), however, falls annually in the western hill country of Koszeg and Sopron in the Little Plain. Getting adequate, clean drinking water is often difficult in the drier areas that are far from rivers.

Despite this uneven pattern of water distribution, Hungary has therapeutic springs known worldwide for their healing properties. More than five hundred mineral and medicinal springs make the nation a popular health resort destination.

HIGH AND LOW LANDS

Hungary is not mountainous although, many centuries ago, the still-young earth muscled up a row of rock formations. These are known as the Bakony and Vertes mountains. They are not very

Left: The Danube Bend at Visegrad   Right: The Citadel on Castle Hill in Visegrad

high, barely 1,000 feet (305 meters). The Matra Mountains along the far northern border with Slovakia are a bit higher. The country's tallest peak, the sheer-sided Kekes, is here, and rises 3,330 feet (1,015 meters).

THE DANUBE BEND

The lowest point in Hungary is near Szeged in the far south, at 259 feet (79 meters) above sea level.

The most picturesque spot in Hungary is the Danube Bend in the north, where the mighty river turns south to cut the nation in half. This stretch of water is only about fourteen miles (twenty-three kilometers) long. At one time it formed the *limes Romanus,* the outer frontier of the Roman Empire. Seldom did any of the usually brave Roman legionnaires cross into barbarian territory on the opposite bank. They felt it was foolhardy, as if they would

Left: Goulash is a hearty stew of beef, potatoes, and paprika.
Right: A shepherd keeping warm on the puszta

be stepping off the end of the world. For the Romans there was nothing beyond the Danube but savages, monsters, horrible weather, starvation, thirst, and unknown calamities.

At the Danube Bend is the ancient city of Visegrad, once the seat of Hungarian royalty. Kings and queens appreciated the scenic beauty as well as the strategic importance of the district. Today, ordinary Hungarians have built numerous summer cottages along the Danube Bend. The stretch of river has become a recreational playground.

In olden times, however, only royalty had the opportunity to enjoy the scenery. The peasants had to contend with making a living. A definite caste, or social, system evolved around herding the animals. At the top of the ladder were the *csikosok*, the horsemen; next came the *gulyasok*, the cowherds; third in status were the *pasztorok*, the shepherds. At the lowly bottom were the swineherds, the *kanaszok*. (The word *goulash* comes from the gulyasok, who made a delicious stew of potatoes, beef, and paprika.)

A stork's nest atop a power pole (left) and a cowherd with his puli (right)

ANIMALS

Also keeping constant watch on the herds and flocks are the Hungarian *pulis*, a breed of rough-coated dogs that have adapted well to rugged life on the plains. The small, tough animals are seldom seen outside the puszta and are important helpers for the herdsmen.

Coexisting with the domestic animals are wild cats, deer, bears, foxes, and flocks of birds. Herons, hawks, and plovers fill the sky. Villagers encourage storks to nest in the chimneys, hoping that the ungainly, long-billed birds will bring good luck.

Fresh air and gardens (left) are as important to Hungarians as are restoring old village cottages (right).

HOUSING

In the small towns, old peasant houses surround central courtyards, with only a window or two facing the sunny side of the street. High wooden fences between the buildings present a solid wall along the highways.

In a typical Hungarian farmhouse, bedrooms are toward the front, with a sitting room in the center, and the kitchen in the back. Fat geese, stuffed with corn to enlarge their livers, strut everywhere. When the geese are killed, the livers make excellent eating. Hungarian goose liver pate is prized in the world's great restaurants.

Many of the more remote houses are still without electricity. But that doesn't bother some of today's young urban Hungarians. They buy the old houses at very low prices and convert them into vacation cottages. On weekends there are always streams of autos from the towns. City dwellers are attracted by fresh air and the opportunity to have their own fruit trees and vegetable gardens.

Ruins of an ancient Roman town near Budapest

Chapter 3

FROM THE SEVEN TRIBES COMES A NATION

In 1965, archaeologists in Transdanubia discovered a man's skull believed to date back 500,000 years. It was eventually placed in the National Museum in Budapest. The number of other artifacts and bones collected at the site on the Vertes Plateau near Tatabanya showed that humans, or humanlike creatures, must have considered ancient Hungary a good place to live. Remains of similar prehistoric people have also been found in caves in the Bukk Mountains and near Lake Balaton.

More than 1,500 years ago, Roman soldiers wrote about a Celtic tribe called the Eravisci who roamed Transdanubia during the reign of Augustus. The region was then called Pannonia. Several Hungarian cities, such as Esztergom and Gyor, originated as Roman military camps, built to protect the far eastern reaches of the mighty empire. However, the Celtic Eravisci did not make much of a ripple in history.

THE MAGYARS

A tidal wave of eastern warriors came next: Huns, Avars, Lombards, and Slavs, and finally, a warlike Asiatic people who

Arrival of the Magyars in Hungary

originated in the steppes, or plains, of central Russia. The strongest tribe among them were the Megyers, whose name eventually became Magyar or Magyars, the term now applied to Hungarians and their language.

The Magyars were fabled archers and hired themselves as mercenaries to any chief or prince rich enough to pay them. These excellent horsemen could gallop while standing in their stirrups. They could even fire their bows backward. One of their favorite tactics was to charge and then quickly retreat, drawing the enemy after them. When their opponents got close, the Magyars would attack them again. They were so fierce that many frightened rulers simply gave gold to the Magyars so they would be left alone. Yet by the ninth century, even these warrior people began to settle down and grow crops.

On-ogurs, from which the word Hungarian was eventually derived, traditionally meant "Ten Arrows." It indicated the tribes that belonged to a federation of Magyars who controlled the Danube valley. Seven of these tribes joined forces under an elected prince.

Left: The election of Almos, the first chief of the Seven Tribes. Right: Arpad, the son of Almos and second chief

The first chief of the Seven Tribes was Almos. The next chief was his son, Arpad, under whose direction the pagan Seven Tribes took up their bows and attacked the eastern borders of Christian Europe.

PRINCE OTTO

However, the Seven Tribes were eventually defeated by the German Prince Otto at the Battle of Lechfeld in 955. Otto demanded that the tribes settle down. Christian missionaries visited the various tribes and converted many of the people. One of the bravest of these priests was later called St. Adalbert. He convinced Geza, Arpad's great-grandson, to accept the Roman Catholic faith. Geza was then chief of the Seven Tribes. Adalbert became good friends with Geza's son, Stephen, and converted him as well.

ST. STEPHEN

When Stephen became leader of the Seven Tribes, he made his followers become Catholic even though many were reluctant to

A bronze equestrian statue of St. Stephen in Budapest

convert. Before Stephen could consolidate his power, he had to put down pagan revolts.

In 1000, Stephen became Hungary's first king. He then abolished the tribal system and set up a centralized government, encouraging foreigners to serve in his court. Among them were English soldiers of fortune, Italian artists, and French scholars. Although Stephen's court was known for its international outlook, he demanded that the native Magyar language be spoken so the traditions of his people would be maintained. Forty-four years after his death, Stephen was canonized, becoming the patron saint of Hungary. His feast day is August 20.

The symbol of Hungary is St. Stephen's crown, which was never actually worn by the beloved king. It was made about one hundred years after his death. Yet the crown, and the authority that it represents, has been fought over by rivals through the centuries. During the last days of World War II, Hungarian refugees brought the crown to the United States where it remained locked in Fort Knox until 1978, when it was returned to Hungary. St. Stephen's crown continues to be the outward symbol of the nation's existence.

ST. GELLERT

King Stephen's one son, Imre, was tragically killed in a hunting accident when he was eighteen years old. Therefore, when Stephen died, he had no natural successor. Arguments raged over who should take over the throne. The eventual heir was an Italian, the son of Stephen's sister. This poor fellow was not well received by the Hungarians. They revolted, led by some of the pagans who had escaped Stephen's earlier Christianizing efforts. Many priests were killed in the uprising, among them the future Saint Gellert, the first bishop of Hungary.

According to legend, Gellert was stuffed into a barrel studded with nails and tossed over a cliff into the raging Danube. He, of course, died. The site is now the tree-shrouded Gellert Hill park on the Buda side of the river in the Hungarian capital. A massive statue there honors the brave bishop, St. Gellert.

A SUCCESSION OF RULERS

A succession of weak rulers followed, and the petty nobles grew more powerful and rich at the expense of the general population. The princes often ignored royal dictates and did what they wanted. In 1222, the lesser nobles forced King Andrew II to sign the Golden Bull, or proclamation, that further limited the king's power and established the beginnings of a Parliament.

This situation was exploited in 1241, when the Mongols roared out of the east and easily crushed the unorganized Hungarians. The Hungarian King Bela IV and his royal family barely escaped as the rough-riding Asian warriors destroyed everything. A terrible famine followed in the wake of their rampage.

After the Mongols departed, Bela returned to find only devastation. Poems from this era say that barely a stone stood upon a stone. Like his predecessor, Stephen, Bela turned to the outside world for help in rebuilding his shattered nation. As before, foreigners came to help. Soon Hungary was even more powerful than it had ever been. Rulers of other countries sent their children to study in the wealthy Hungarian court because it was noted for its intellectual achievements.

Hungary's location on the trade routes between the Baltic Sea on the north and the Black Sea on the south guaranteed it a privileged economic position. Besides, during the Middle Ages, Hungarian mines provided two-thirds of Europe's gold. Both factors contributed to the growing wealth of the king and the nobles. In addition, Hungarian silversmiths were considered among the best in the world at the time. They traveled everywhere, selling their skillfully produced items.

This magnificent period lasted only a hundred years or so. Another problem, one that would affect all of Europe, was gathering strength on Hungary's southern borders.

The mighty Ottoman (Turkish) Empire was expanding. Its fast-moving scouts probed deeply into Hungarian territory, assessing the defenses. Instead of increasing their fortifications, the Hungarian kings argued with the nobles. Both were squandering their fortunes on elaborate castles and pleasures far from the troubled borders. They had not learned much from the Mongol attacks. In 1387, Sigismund of Luxembourg became king of Hungary after marrying the daughter of one of the previous Hungarian kings. His duties as Holy Roman emperor and king of Bohemia also kept him very busy.

Janos Hunyadi

JANOS HUNYADI

Seeing a weak Hungary and an ill-prepared Europe, the Ottoman Turks stormed into the Balkans. The Turks, however, didn't expect to find the Hungarian Janos Hunyadi waiting for them. An excellent strategist, Hunyadi often defeated the Turks. His legendary fighting ability and statesmanship helped him become a Hungarian folk hero. Instead of depending on an army of pampered nobles and their soft courtiers, Hunyadi forged a tough mercenary army responsible only to him.

Hunyadi copied the tactics of the early Magyars by drawing out the Turkish cavalry far from their infantry and then ambushing the horsemen. As a result, the Hungarians and their allies could safely attack the main Turkish army on its flanks and rear. This method worked very well in many bloody confrontations.

As the Turkish pressure increased, Hunyadi could not continue his early successes. At the Battle of Varna in 1444, King Vladislas of Hungary was killed and Hunyadi had to retreat. But the Turkish commander wept when he looked at the battlefield, littered with the bodies of more than thirty-two thousand of his own dead soldiers. He supposedly said that he would not be able to afford many more victories like that one. The climax of the running war between the Ottomans and Hunyadi came at the Battle of Belgrade in 1456, when the Turks were finally repulsed.

Hunyadi died a few months later, not in battle but from the plague. Even his respectful enemies, the Turks, praised him, saying, "The Lion of Hungary is dead."

Upon hearing of Hunyadi's unexpected death, the Roman Catholic pope, Calixtus III, ordered that all church bells in Europe be rung at noon. The prelate wanted to honor the soldier's memory and to commemorate the victory at Belgrade. The tradition remains today.

MATTHIAS

Janos Hunyadi's son, Matthias Corvinus, was proclaimed king on New Year's Day in 1458. Matthias was only eighteen years old, but had learned a great deal while fighting alongside his father. In addition to being an expert warrior, he was well read and highly literate. In fact, some of his books are still exhibited at the National Museum.

Unlike most other kings of his day, Matthias was concerned about the peasants. He often disguised himself and wandered about the countryside to learn firsthand what was happening. Yet he also was very tough. Like his father, Matthias hired a mercenary force made up mostly of hefty, determined Germans and Czechs that earned the dreaded name of "The Black Army." In addition to keeping the Ottoman Turks at bay, Matthias used his loyal troops to control the unruly Hungarian barons. No one dared oppose him. His coat of arms was an angry raven.

When Matthias died, the usual arguments erupted over who would earn the right to wear the crown of St. Stephen. Unfortunately, as in preceding generations, a succession of unfit kings grabbed power. They hiked taxes and made life generally miserable for the peasants.

THE PEASANTS REVOLT

In 1514, a great military expedition was launched against the ruling class. Thousands of Hungarian peasants joined. The barons and princes were outraged that their field workers, craftsmen, and laborers were revolting. So they demanded that the army disband. The new soldiers refused. In their anger, they attacked the vast feudal estates. They burned mansions and massacred many of the short-sighted nobility.

The revolution was led by a small landowner named Gyorgy Dozsa. The peasants were no match for the better-trained royal forces, however, and the rebellion was crushed. More than seventy thousand peasants were executed in retaliation for their part in the revolt. Ridiculed as "King of the Peasants," Dozsa died by being placed on a red-hot iron throne, with a heated crown placed on his head. Dozsa became another major Hungarian legend after he was martyred.

TURKISH RULE

After this calamity, even more trouble was brewing for Hungary. Led by booming kettledrums, the mighty Turkish army was on the march again. Another confrontation was inevitable.

The Hungarians were defeated at the Battle of Mohacs on August 29, 1526, a dark day in the history of the tormented nation. This allowed the Turks to swarm north through the soft underbelly of the wounded nation. They swiftly captured and destroyed the court at Buda, initiating 150 years of Turkish rule.

Tens of thousands of Hungarians were enslaved and hauled in chains back to Turkish territory. Few escaped. With no one to tend the land, fields were soon overgrown. The unchecked rivers flooded and spread disease. The marshes and sandy wasteland that resulted became known as the puszta. Many Hungarians became Muslims, like their masters.

At this time, Hungary was about three times its current size. The Turks controlled the southern and eastern plains. Led by the Hapsburgs, a land-hungry Austria moved in on Hungary's western territories. In the north, along the Carpathian Mountains, an ongoing war raged for years between the Turks, the Austrians, and what few Hungarian nobles remained free. Only Transylvania was relatively unscathed, protected by fog-shrouded mountains and deep crevasses that slowed the movement of armies.

Before the Turkish invasion, there were an estimated 4,500,000 Hungarians. By the time Hungarian lands were recaptured, fewer than 2,500,000 Magyars were left. Buda was finally recaptured by Christian forces in 1686. But Hungary replaced one oppressor with another. The Austrians strode into the political vacuum and made Hungary its province. In 1703, an eight-year rebellion broke out against the Austrians, led by Prince Ferenc Rakoczi II of Transylvania.

The lightly armed and ill-prepared peasants were called the *kuruc*, in honor of the crucifixes worn by Gyorgy Dozsa's peasants.

Prince Ferenc Rakoczi II (left) and Maria Theresa (right)

The kuruc were patriotic and brave, but that was not enough when charging headlong at blasting cannons. Naturally, the revolt was bloodily crushed.

MARIA THERESA OF AUSTRIA

In 1740, Maria Theresa of Austria became queen of Hungary. She tried to rule wisely and built many schools and universities. However, the Hungarian nobles feared an educated populace. They complained loudly over any reforms that would threaten their exalted position on the huge estates. Therefore, Hungary remained basically agricultural. The Austrians did not do much to improve the living conditions of the people. They preferred to keep the nation as backward as possible to prevent uprisings. The little freedom they allowed was only for the advantage of the barons and princes.

Yet there was still an undercurrent of unrest. Many starving peasants became outlaws, causing a great deal of trouble for the authorities. While they weren't exactly Robin Hoods, robbing the rich to give to the poor, the brigands were usually fed and hidden by sympathetic friends. Anyone who could harass the Austrians was considered a hero.

Two men emerged as leaders of a broadening reform movement. One was Count Istvan Szechenyi. The count was considered a renegade by his fellow nobles. They were shocked when he offered his income for an entire year to set up an academy of arts and sciences. At one time, he spoke to the Hungarian Diet, the Parliament permitted by the Austrians. Instead of speaking in the official court language of Latin, Szechenyi spoke to the representatives in Magyar, the people's tongue.

Under his insistence, the first bridge was built across the Danube River between Buda and Pest. Szechenyi convinced Scottish engineer Adam Clark to construct the famous Szechenyi Bridge. Everybody was glad that the span was built, but the nobles were outraged that Szechenyi made them pay a toll to cross, the same as the peasants. They thought they should be exempt. But Szechenyi remained firm and everyone paid the toll.

Clark's engineering achievement is still honored in Budapest. The roadway at the end of the bridge on the Buda bank is called Adam Clark Circle. The bridge was destroyed by the retreating Nazis during World War II, but rebuilt exactly as it was during the 1840s.

Another Hungarian leader emerged about the same time. Lajos Kossuth was a lawyer, lecturer, and orator who traveled around

Lajos Kossuth (left) and Sandor Petofi (right)

Hungary urging an end to Austrian rule. Throughout Europe, many other reform leaders looked to Kossuth as an inspiration.

His ideas caught on among university students who took over a printing office so they could publish uncensored newspapers. This act is considered the beginning of the Hungarian War for Freedom. It lasted only a year but the fighting changed the course of Hungarian nationalism.

Many brilliant young men and women fought for Hungarian freedom, including poet Sandor Petofi. A number of these eager liberal thinkers formed a representative parliamentary government in 1848. Instead of uniting and building a strong foundation for a new government, however, they argued over policy. Despite their problems, the Parliament did manage to draft a declaration of independence for Hungary.

Austrians storming the castle at Budapest

EMPEROR FRANZ JOSEPH

An army recruited by Kossuth was able to initially defeat the occupying Austrians. However, lack of support by the other leaders of the revolution doomed his subsequent efforts. The new emperor of the Austrians, a tough-minded, eighteen-year-old named Franz Joseph, was determined to crush the revolt by any means. He called on the Russian tsar to attack Hungary from the east, while he sent in a powerful Austrian army from the west. Hit from both sides at once, Hungarian resistance collapsed like a balloon. The decimated Hungarian army laid down its arms on August 13, 1849. In the aftermath, the vengeful Austrians hanged thirteen Hungarian generals in a single day. Kossuth barely escaped. His flight carried him through Turkey, England, the United States, and finally to Italy, where he died in exile, far from his beloved country.

Chapter 4

DARK DAYS LEAD
TO LIGHT

There were grim days ahead for Hungary in the turbulent 1850s. Kossuth and his revolutionary friends were dead, imprisoned, or in exile. The army was tightly controlled by the Austrians, who emphasized allegiance to the empire rather than the nation. A rigid police state, with imperial spies everywhere, existed. Newspapers and magazines were censored, and patriotic meetings were outlawed. Hungarians were afraid to speak of the War for Freedom because they might be arrested for treason.

Alexander Bach, the Austrian minister of the interior, was responsible for overseeing the new Hungary. He was very strict and ruthless. His name is still vilified in Hungary today. Despite the political climate, the period after the revolution led to the development of a booming economy and stability for the battle-weary nation. At least there was peace, allowing people to get on with earning a living.

The repression did not last forever. Within a decade, the Austrians were willing to forgive small sins as long as the Hungarians paid their taxes. By 1859, Austria was more concerned with controlling its outer provinces, and it slowly loosened its iron grip on Hungary. It was easier to placate the Hungarians than keep them stirred up and angry.

In this era, Hungary again demonstrated that it was a crossroads nation, a land of many cultures. Thousands of Germans, Croats, Serbs, Romanians, and other nationalities filtered into southern Hungary. Under the protective mantle of the Austrian empire, they sought security and prosperity on new farms. They usually joined citizens of the same ethnic background who had come to Hungary generations earlier. That first wave of emigrants arrived after the bloody Turkish invasion had decimated the local Magyar population. Many of these non-Hungarian enclaves remain today. One well-known Hungarian town is Hajos, populated by Catholic Germans called *Donauschwabens* (Danube Swabians), who retain their original dialect, folk costumes, and winemaking skills.

THE COMPROMISE OF 1867

Finally, the Austrians made a major political concession that delighted Hungarian subjects. This was the Compromise of 1867, an agreement that gave a great deal of internal independence to Hungary. The agreement was the brainchild of Ferenc Deak, a Hungarian parliamentarian. Deak's fellow citizens nicknamed him "The Wise Man of the Country" for his perception and ability to maneuver them out from under Austrian domination.

Austria's Franz Joseph was made monarch of what was called the Austro-Hungarian Empire. With bands playing and flags waving, the thirty-seven-year-old ruler was crowned in Budapest's beautiful Matthias Church. Church bells rang out

Franz Joseph (left) and Ferenc Deak (right)

loudly across Buda and Pest as he became king of Hungary and emperor of Austria.

Manufacturing began in earnest in the 1870s, although the nation was still primarily dependent on agriculture. Starving peasants flocked to the cities seeking work. Initially, most industries were tied to processing farm products. First there were flour mills, then foul-smelling tanneries for treating leather, followed by construction of breweries that scented the air with the sweetness of hops.

There still was not a large middle class. A few Hungarians were very rich, living in elaborate villas. Most were extremely poor, living in dingy city tenements or in squalid country farmhouses. The Parliament at this time was divided into an Upper House and a House of Deputies. A hereditary title was necessary to get a seat in the Upper House. Usually only wealthy men could buy a seat in the House of Deputies. Generally, neither body did much for the common folk. Laws were passed that favored the aristocracy and the landed gentry.

To enforce their decrees, a special police force called the *pandoors* was organized. Grim-faced sergeants led platoons of men in all-black uniforms around the countryside, on the alert for anyone talking against the government. The ordinary Hungarian didn't think much of this. It seemed as if one oppressor had replaced another, but what made it worse was that the pandoors were striking fear in their own countrymen everywhere they roamed.

The aristocratic Hungarians thought it was beneath their dignity to work. They lived off the money earned from their agricultural estates. The vacuum in the trading and professional class was filled by the Jews, who were very industrious. They became doctors, teachers, shopkeepers, bankers, and lawyers. Despite their achievements, or because of them, they were often victims of discrimination. Yet the Jews were very active financial supporters of the War for Freedom. They were patriotic, but some military units refused to enlist young Jewish men. Despite the restrictions, the hardworking Jews were among the wealthiest Hungarians by the 1900s. Many converted to Christianity and intermarried with the gentry.

While the Hungarian countryside remained in poverty, Budapest was the crown jewel of the nation. The cities of Buda, Pest, and Obuda were united in 1873, creating an explosion of construction, commerce, and artistic excitement. Yet behind the glittering facade were crowded slums, rampant with disease and starvation.

When Hungary celebrated its one-thousandth anniversary in 1896, all that was forgotten. Fireworks, friendliness, and festivals were everywhere. Even the poor enjoyed the pomp and circumstance. The anniversary ushered in a golden age for

An artist's conception of the assassination of Archduke Franz Ferdinand of Austria

Hungary. Arts, science, and industry bloomed. Another reform movement began, under the aegis of the Society of Social Sciences. Its members were among the leading intellectuals of the day. Radicals, middle of the roaders, and conservatives joined. Coffeehouses in Pest were crowded with poets, scholars, and political activists arguing over the best means to shake Hungary out of its slow, restrictive ways.

WORLD WAR I

This breath of fresh air ended abruptly on June 28, 1914, when Franz Joseph's heir, the Archduke Franz Ferdinand of Austria, was assassinated at Sarajevo. The murder was the final act in a long road of mistrust, militarism, and misplaced patriotism that led to the horrors of World War I. Because of their political ties to the monarchy, the Hungarians were drawn into the conflict on the side of the Austrians and the Germans, a fact that few Magyars actually relished.

After a brief period of flag waving and high spirits, the war ground down to a long battle. There was no glory to be seen as the winding columns of torn and wounded soldiers straggled home.

By the end of World War I, more than 380,000 Hungarians had died in battle. Many people wondered why they had gone to war in the first place.

At this time, other circumstances outside their control affected the Hungarians as well. Emperor Franz Joseph died on November 21, 1916. The new king of Hungary was Franz Joseph's grandnephew Karl, who took the name Charles IV. Charles allowed greater freedom to the many Hungarian political parties that had sprung up during the war. Since he had to concentrate on the battlefront, Charles was unable to control the different ethnic elements throughout the empire that wanted to break away. This ferment soon had grave consequences.

Second, there was a revolution in Russia, and Tsar Nicholas II abdicated on March 15, 1917. His stepping down from authority and eventual execution initiated a scramble for power in Hungary's huge neighbor. Among those seeking to gain control of Russia were the Bolsheviks, later to be known as Communists, under the leadership of Vladimir Lenin. The Bolsheviks eventually defeated their rivals and assumed total power over Russia.

By the autumn of 1918, it was obvious that the end of World War I was near. The entire Austro-Hungarian army disintegrated as the Slovaks, Serbs, Croats, Czechs, and other nationalities in the empire threw down their weapons and broke for home.

HUNGARY BECOMES AN EMPIRE

On October 25, a Hungarian National Council was formed to handle the day-to-day functions of government. Charles IV stepped down from the Hungarian throne soon afterward. Free at last from Austrian influence, the Hungarian Parliament declared

Count Mihaly Karolyi (center) on a visit to Budapest in about 1945

that the country was a republic. Count Mihaly Karolyi was named prime minister. By November 1918, the war was officially ended.

At the good news, happy Hungarians cheered in the streets, waved banners, and wept. They thought it was the dawning of a new, peaceful era. Instead, it became a dismal time. No economic or political help came from the democratic nations that had won the war. They ignored the fact that Hungary's industry was in shambles and that most of its ex-soldiers were out of work. The Hungarians did not know which way to turn.

COMMUNISM GAINS STRENGTH

Hungarian Communists gained strength in the turmoil that followed. The party was led by Bela Kun, an ex-prisoner of war and a journalist who had a gift for oratory. Since the West did not come to their aid, many Hungarians looked east, toward the new regime in Russia that later would be called the Soviet Union. They believed that the Soviet Communists there could help solve their troubles.

Karolyi's government had freed Kun from prison. He had been jailed for starting riots. A Republic of Councils, or Soviets, was formed on March 21, 1919, with Kun as commissar of foreign affairs. He actually headed the government, which lasted only 133 days. But during that time, farms of more than 140 acres (57 hectares) were taken over by the government, the eight-hour workday was established, compulsory social insurance started, and voting rights for all citizens was permitted.

COLLAPSE OF SOVIET-STYLE REGIME

The rest of Europe was terrified of Kun's government. The Europeans blockaded the frontier and refused to let any food or reconstruction supplies enter Hungary. With the aid of the French, military forces from Romania, Czechoslovakia, and Serbia invaded Hungary and soon stormed into Budapest. Kun fled with his associates, and the short-lived Soviet-style regime collapsed. Gangs of toughs, many of them former officers in the imperial army, roamed through Hungary. "The Whites," as they were called, shot anyone they suspected of favoring the Kun government. In the frenzy, thousands of Jews were murdered as well.

Most of the battered Hungarian army never liked Kun and his Communist ideals. After some half-hearted attempts to keep the invaders at bay, the army surrendered. Karoly Huszar became president under a new government that voided all regulations made during the regimes of Karolyi and Kun.

Rear Admiral Nicolas Horthy was responsible for organizing the forces that caused the collapse of the Kun reign. Late in 1919, Horthy became the head of a conservative government, becoming regent of the Hungarian Kingdom.

TREATY OF TRIANON

Western Europe wanted more revenge, even after it crushed the Kun government. The Treaty of Trianon in June 1920, part of World War I peace settlements, took away almost two-thirds of what had been pre-war Hungary. More than three million Magyars subsequently found themselves citizens of the enlarged states of Romania, Austria, Czechoslovakia, and Yugoslavia.

Fleeing back to Hungary were about 350,000 ex-officers and soldiers of "The Whites," as well as landowners and businessmen. They received many favors from Horthy and his government because their conservative support was highly valued.

WORLD WAR II

Over the next twenty-five years, Horthy's regime grew stronger, and closely allied itself to Adolf Hitler's Nazi Germany. When World War II broke out in 1938, Hungary entered on the side of its German friends. The country hoped this alliance would help regain its lost provinces, but it was a false dream.

Hitler took control of Hungary in March 1944. The Nazis rounded up Jews and sent them to labor or concentration camps. Horthy was arrested and replaced by Ferenc Szalasi, the head of the Arrow Cross, a band of fanatical Hungarian fascists who were similar to the German Nazis.

During the war, more than 400,000 Hungarian Jews were deported to death camps and subsequently murdered. Under Szalasi, the reign of terror intensified, but Raoul Wallenberg, a Swedish diplomat in Hungary, saved the lives of 100,000 Jews by hiding them or giving them forged Swedish passports. When the

Soviet Red army swept over Hungary late in 1944, Wallenberg disappeared and presumably was killed by the Communists.

RETURN TO COMMUNISM

By the time the Soviet Union completed its occupation of Hungary on April 4, 1945, the country was again in ruins. Its buildings were crumpled shells, bridges were destroyed, and hundreds of thousands of Hungarians were dead. Yet even before the war dragged to a gruesome halt, the Soviets had already set up their own Provisional Hungarian National Government, with Hungarian Communists in charge. Heading the government was Matyas Rakosi, the son of a country shopkeeper who had held a position in the Kun government before it fell.

The Soviet army still occupied Hungary as "liberators." A secret police was organized. These dreaded officers were the AVO, or State Security Department. The police effectively silenced any opponents of the new regime.

Hungarian Communists supported by the Soviets gained control of the government after the 1947 elections. They nationalized all industry and farms the next year. Even landowners who only had a few acres were forced to turn over their plots. Many church groups spoke out against this confiscation and growing police terror. In an effort to halt the protests, the AVO arrested Jozsef Cardinal Mindszenty, head of the Roman Catholics in Hungary. The Communists claimed that the prelate was plotting to overthrow the government and reinstall the monarchy.

Next, Lutheran Bishop Lajos Ordas was caught in the dragnet. Other religious leaders also disappeared into prison. No one was

Jozsef Cardinal Mindszenty (left) during his trial, and Matyas Rakosi (right)

safe; schoolchildren reported on their parents, and neighbors were afraid of each other.

Hungary evolved into a Soviet substate. The head of the Soviet government, Josef Stalin, was praised and applauded. His picture was everywhere. The old Hungarian coat of arms was replaced by one that looked like one of the Soviet republics. A red star was placed in the center of the green, white, and red Hungarian flag. Western films and books were banned.

Instead of prospering, Hungary stumbled along from three-year plan to five-year plan in agriculture and industry. The early 1950s were drab and dreary. There were lengthy lines for all sorts of goods, from bread to soap, but no one could complain. Hungary was intended to be a workshop for the good of the Soviet Union, with little thought being given to the Hungarian people themselves.

Young people, however, received many privileges. Parks and playgrounds were built, free trips were organized, and castles were turned into youth hostels. A special railroad, run by a

Members of the Young Pioneers (left) and the Young Pioneer Railway (right)

children's organization called the Young Pioneers, was established in the hills of Budapest. It was a tourist attraction, where children acted as conductors, brakemen, and ticket takers.

PREMIER IMRE NAGY

Stalin died on March 5, 1953. A succession of other Soviet leaders who did not share his views came to power. They forced Rakosi, as first secretary of the Hungarian Communist party, to give up some of his power and named Imre Nagy premier. Nagy, also a dedicated Communist, was then president of the National Assembly, which had replaced the pre-war Parliament.

When Nagy gave his first speech as premier, he loudly criticized Rakosi's government. Nagy even had some of the top AVO officers imprisoned, and he supported the release of Cardinal Mindszenty.

Hungarian revolutionaries, carrying a white flag with a red cross marked with blood, speed through Budapest in 1956.

However, in 1955, Rakosi sought help from other Soviet friends, who encouraged him to purge Nagy. Although the premier was removed from office, his reforms had gone on too long. Many political prisoners, set free under Nagy, told others about the terrible things the AVO had done under Rakosi's direction. Writers, such as Tibor Dery, spoke out against the government's excesses, although they were still proud of being Communists.

THE REVOLUTION OF 1956

In March 1956, Communist party officials told Rakosi that the Hungarian people no longer trusted him, and the ever-present Soviets ordered him to resign. But his replacement, Erno Gero, was also detested by the Hungarians. On October 23, students in Budapest marched on the government radio station to demand more reforms. Gero ordered police to fire on the crowd, thus turning a calm, peaceful protest into a revolution.

Stalin's statue lies in the streets of Budapest

Opposition spread immediately. People bravely took to the streets and proclamations were aired. Hungarian military units gave their support to the crowds, handing out weapons and even leading the marches. A huge statue of Stalin in Budapest's main city park was torn down amid cheers from a huge crowd. Several small towns were taken over by the rebels. Demonstrations and fighting erupted in Debrecen, Pecs, Szeged, and Miskolc. Red stars, the symbols of the Communist government, were torn down and party offices were burned.

The occupying Soviet army immediately responded. Columns of tanks rolled into Budapest late in the day on October 24. They were greeted by jeers of "Russians, go home." From the protection of side streets and alleys, youngsters dashed out to block the tanks. Once halted, the tanks were prime targets for Molotov cocktails, homemade gasoline bombs. These running firefights turned Hungary's major cities into war zones. As one eyewitness said, "Budapest's schoolboys defeated the Red army."

A group of revolutionaries hold a flag with the cross of St. Stephen as they stand on a captured Soviet tank (left), but more tanks (right) keep arriving.

But there was a price. Hundreds of civilians and soldiers on both sides were killed as the fighting intensified. By October 27, there was civil war. The Soviets, gradually realizing the mistakes made by Rakosi and Gero, gave in to a few of the rebels' demands. They fired many of the ruling Hungarian Communists, a token action since most had fled the capital and were in hiding.

The eager Hungarians wanted more reforms. They urged a return of the multiparty form of government, along with freedom of worship. They wanted the Soviet soldiers removed from Hungarian soil. They agreed, however, with public ownership of manufacturing and with collective agriculture. On November 3, a newly formed cabinet pulled together many political elements, including non-Communists.

The Soviets promised to leave Hungary, but had a change of heart as the demands for reform increased. They feared any changes in the Hungarian political scene might lead to a drift away from the communistic system. Subsequently, Hungary's brief glimmer of hope and freedom ended on the night of November 3, when Budapest was attacked with renewed fury. However, it took the Soviets weeks before they totally squelched the rebellion. At least five thousand Hungarians and an untold number of Soviet soldiers died. About forty thousand persons were jailed, and fifteen thousand were executed, including Premier Nagy. Two hundred thousand Hungarians fled to the West. Janos Kadar, another Communist functionary, was named premier. Because he came to power backed by the muscle of the Soviet army, Kadar was called the "Butcher of Budapest." Later, however, he became more popular because he slowly edged Hungary away from the rigid Soviet-style Communist system. He called the hard days of 1956 a "national tragedy." But the Soviet army became an occupying force on Hungarian soil.

AFTERMATH OF THE REVOLUTION

After the revolution, the Hungarians had to coexist with their giant neighbor. In exchange for peace, the country was given certain special economic privileges unlike those in other Communist states. In Hungary's "goulash" Communism, some private businesses are allowed, factory managers were given more say in their work, and farmers could sell their own produce.

The political situation seemed more relaxed, at least on the surface. The government allowed Hungarians to listen to Radio Free Europe. Many refugees who fled to the West in 1956 returned home and were not punished. Tourism was encouraged, and lofty new hotels sprang up all over the country. Vacationing Hungarians were able to visit Western countries.

But Hungarians still wanted to be free. In 1988 some people

In Budapest, a variety of produce is available in the market. The glass walls of the Hilton Hotel reflect Matyas (Matthias) Church (right).

began to say that the Communist system needed to be changed. They said the Communist system didn't work. They wanted a political party to be responsible to the people. Separate political groups began to appear.

In 1988, Janos Kadar, who had been the party leader since 1956, was replaced. Karoly Grosz became the new party leader.

In 1989, great changes came to Eastern Europe and to Hungary. The name of the country was changed from Hungarian People's Republic to the Republic of Hungary. Political leaders agreed to pass laws that would allow free and democratic elections in 1990. In those elections in March and April 1990, the Communist party was defeated.

A new democratic government took power. The Soviet army left Hungary, and Hungarians were finally free to govern themselves.

A view from Fisherman's Bastion—
In the picture above, Pest is on the left of the Danube and Buda on the right.
Below left: Automobile traffic in downtown Budapest
Below right: Renovated homes in the Castle Hill district

Chapter 5

HUNGARY'S REGAL CITIES

BUDAPEST

Budapest is a lively city. Bright neon lights, automobiles, crowded parks, elaborate architecture, and a thousand years of history make it a cosmopolitan mecca. At night, floodlights beam on the Castle Hill district of Buda, illuminating the Royal Palace and the plaza called Fisherman's Bastion behind the fabled Matyas (Matthias) Church. From a promenade along the rim of the plaza, it is easy to see the differences between hilly Buda and the flat Pest sides of the river.

Buda sports pastel-painted buildings, quiet neighborhoods, and huge shade trees. Some of the older buildings are still pockmarked with shell and bullet holes, reminders both of World War II and the Revolution of 1956.

However, in Pest's newer sections, glass, concrete, and steel seem to be the primary construction materials. A row of fancy hotels lines the riverbanks there. Over the past two decades, the

*A park on a quiet autumn afternoon (left),
and a busy sidewalk cafe (right) in Budapest*

multistory accommodations have been built by foreign investors. They know the city is one of Eastern Europe's primary tourist attractions. The Pest banks are more peaceful, with quiet parks and tree-lined walkways. Forgotten are the leather-clad Mongol horsemen who once stood here.

One guidebook calls Budapest the "essence of Hungary." It is a delightful combination of old and new. Budapest is the seat of government, typified by the imposing Parliament and other government buildings. More than two million people live in the capital city's twenty-two districts. The residents have a continental look that matches an ebullient town spirit. Gracious old men wearing white gloves still offer their subway seats to women passengers. Teenagers sport punk rock hairdos and carry boom-box radios.

Budapest brings together all Hungary under "one roof." The most recently annexed suburb in the southern part of the city

*Young girls at a shopping stall where modern casual
clothes are sold (left) and two friends relaxing on a park bench*

used to be a German village. After the Turks were driven away in
the seventeenth century, Germans and Slovaks were brought in to
populate the decimated community. There are still neighborhoods
in Buda where German is spoken rather than Magyar. The
baroque yellow color on the old churches is evidence of Austrian
rule. From their inside perches, ornate cherubs peek down on the
congregations.

Rounded domes of ancient Turkish mosques, usually now
Christian churches or museums, can be seen around the city. On
Castle Hill, a small Turkish cemetery with gravestones topped
with carved turbans has survived a multitude of stormy
generations. Another remnant of those days is the elaborate
Turkish steambath in the shadow of Gellert Hill. The bath is one
of 123 springs within the city. For only a little money, a visitor
can soak for more than an hour in the hot and cold waters. Burly,
knuckle-cracking masseurs knead bodies as if they were great

The exterior of the Opera House in Budapest (left) and a performance of Bela Bartok's opera, Bluebeard's Castle

lumps of bread dough. It's a relief to stumble loose limbed into a nearby hall lined with beds for a catnap.

Budapest has been destroyed and rebuilt so often that layers of history are peeled away every time street repairs are made or foundations dug. During the siege of 1686, when the Turks were finally driven from the city, an eyewitness wrote that the burning houses in Buda were like empty skulls glowing with lighted candles planted inside.

The Nazi devastation at the end of World War II was worse. Adolf Hitler, the German leader, wanted his troops to make a final stand in Budapest. The Nazis and their Hungarian allies fought bitterly. By the time the Soviet army crashed through the enemy defenses, the city was in ruins. It is hard today to believe that many buildings seen now are reconstructions of the originals. The Hungarians were careful to preserve and recreate as much of the old Budapest as possible. For instance, the State Opera house reopened in the mid-1980s after years of painstaking

Above: Mellenary Monument in Heroes' Square
Left: A popular coffeehouse

refurbishment by the country's best craftsmen. Now the seats and boxes are packed for performances of *Bluebeard's Castle* by Bela Bartok and works of other famous Hungarian and international composers.

Monuments to the Soviet Red army rim the hills overlooking the city, where some of the most savage fighting of World War II took place. The towering female statue, called "Liberty," atop Gellert Hill is another symbol of the Soviet victory over the Nazis and Hungarian fascists. Just as impressive is the Mellenary Monument in Heroes' Square. The monument marks the thousandth anniversary of the Magyar conquest of Hungary.

Yet Budapest is more than a city of buildings and memorials. It is a city where small memories stand out. Just as the coffeehouse is still the center of social life, the *dohanybolt* (tobacco shop) is the heart of the neighborhoods. Available for sale are bus tickets, tooth paste, and comic books. Newspapers lie in neat piles

*Matyas (Matthias) Church (left) and
a block of high-rise apartments (above)*

alongside boxes of cigars and stacks of *Ludas,* a weekly humor magazine.

Not far from Gellert Hill is a tiny park with a lake. A sign there says that the pond belongs to the Hungarian Banknote Printing Office.

Budapest's growing population has meant an explosion in housing construction. After World War II, many multi-storied apartments called All-Council homes were built. Block after block of these prefabricated buildings ring the city.

Green buses carry workers from the suburbs into the city. Yellow buses provide transportation around Budapest itself. A bright, swift subway depends on the honor system. Tickets are purchased from vending machines at each stop but are seldom collected by a conductor.

The Hungarian National Gallery and History Museum are housed in Buda Castle (above).
A shopping area (below) in an old section of Budapest

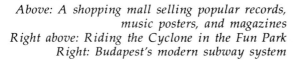

Above: A shopping mall selling popular records,
music posters, and magazines
Right above: Riding the Cyclone in the Fun Park
Right: Budapest's modern subway system

There is always plenty to do in Budapest. The capital has twenty museums, twenty-five major theaters, ten stadiums, over one hundred soccer pitches, and several concert halls. The Budapest City Park with its Zoological Gardens is crammed with families even on weekdays. The nearby Budapest Circus is a favorite with children. It has its own indoor hall so shows can be presented in any kind of weather. The Fun Park has a popular fifty-year-old roller coaster and plenty of up-to-date thrilling rides. Budapest teenagers enjoy the Youth Park near Castle Hill where they can dance and listen to rock concerts. The city is a popular stop for foreign entertainers, who make sure that the Hungarians keep up to date with the latest music from the rest of Europe and the United States.

The Youth Park (above left), the Budapest Zoo (above right), and tour boats
on the Danube (below) are popular forms of recreation.

DUNAUJVAROS

Although Budapest is the crown jewel of Hungarian cities, there are many other important municipalities. A mesh of modern highways leads out from the city, like spokes on a bicycle wheel. Typifying the new Hungary is Dunaujvaros, directly south of the capital some 45 miles (72 kilometers). In 1950, the area was only a sandbar along the Danube shore. Most of the citizens are employed at the Danube Iron Works, the largest foundry in the country, and others work at manufacturing plants.

The stretch of the Danube around Dunaujvaros is a maze of islands and backwaters prized for excellent fishing. International fishing tournaments here have attracted anglers who appreciate the challenge.

The average age of the Dunaujvaros citizen is around thirty-five years old. To accommodate the many young families who live there, the city has about twenty-two kindergartens, eight primary schools, and three secondary schools. A technical college trains engineers and other specialists, many of whom will eventually work in the iron mill.

KECSKEMET

The Great Plains hold several of Hungary's other major cities. Kecskemet is midway between the Danube and Tisza rivers, about fifty-four miles (eighty-seven kilometers) southeast of Budapest.

Kecskemet is the center of apricot growing in Hungary, with distilleries for making brandy and factories for jams and jellies. Before the harvest, orchards appear to be basking in a golden glow due to the bright hue of the heavy, juicy fruit.

A sculpture at the Kodaly Music Institute

Kecskemet has had the status of a town since 1368, but it was a settlement for centuries before that. The chiefs of the On-ogur federation assembled their horses and wagons on the plains nearby to plan their western migration.

The large church in the town square is near a former synagogue that is now a lecture hall. Tragically, all the Jews in the city were deported and murdered during World War II. But Kecskemet has a happier history as well.

It is the birthplace of Zoltan Kodaly, a music educator who worked with composer Bela Bartok to save Hungarian folksongs. The Kodaly Music Institute in an old Franciscan monastery is a quiet, relaxing hideaway. The institute is internationally known for its intensive course work and fine lectures. Kodaly believed that all children should learn music to get them in touch with the other arts. His theory is still an important principle advocated throughout the Hungarian school system.

A village on the outskirts of Szeged

SZEGED

Szeged is the cultural and economic heart of southern Hungary. It is on the banks of the Tisza River, which residents jokingly refer to as "a blonde lady" because of its muddy yellow appearance.

The town cathedral, called the Votive Church, has lofty twin towers and is the symbol of the city. Inside the church is a massive organ with 1,040 pipes and five keyboards. When the instrument is played, it seems as if the walls will fall down. Open-air theater and music festivals are often held on the square fronting the church steps.

On the other side of the city is a sad reminder of the past. A dark, shuttered synagogue brings memories of World War II. More than five thousand Jews lived in Szeged before World War II, but only eight hundred survived. Their temple, one of the oldest in Eastern Europe, was used as a storehouse for the German army. The city was liberated by the Soviets on October 11, 1944, just before the Nazis could blow up the historic structure.

Two universities and thirty primary schools ensure that Szeged now looks toward the future. Young people in the latest fashions

Young folk musicians in native costume

fill the streets and belong to folk music clubs. To accommodate the literary set, there seems to be a bookstore on almost every corner. Szeged is a town of parks and open spaces, providing plenty of space for sprawling out with a good book.

PECS

Pecs is estimated to be about 2,000 years old, on the site where the Romans had a major military camp. The first university in Hungary was established here in 1367. The Turks occupied the city for 143 years, filling it with mosques, baths, and minarets. The mosque of Pasha Gazi Kasim remains as a focal point on Szechenyi Square, a great hangout for teens. The mosque was built on the foundation of an old Catholic church, which in turn was constructed on the ruins of a Roman temple. After the Turks departed, the mosque was converted into a Christian church.

Some folk treasures of Hungary are embroidery (above left), folk dances (above right), and painted dishes and pottery (below).

Picking and sorting the red peppers that are used to make Hungary's famous paprika.

KALOCSA

The Folklore House in the city of Kalocsa is a typical peasant home of the early 1900s. The city has since swallowed up the farmland around the house, now used as a museum and cooperative shop for the sale of embroidery. Women in the community are noted for their delicate stitchery on linens, doll clothes, tablecloths, napkins, and handkerchiefs. A troupe of folk dancers regularly performs Magyar dances in the yard behind the buildings. A pole used in a circle dance shows the Turkish influence on the vicinity. A half moon, the symbol of Turkey, is atop the pole that had been dedicated to Deli Baba, the pagan goddess of fertility. The pole now supposedly honors the "patron" of embroidering.

The Spice Pepper Museum in Kalocsa is the only museum in the world honoring paprika, a fiery pepper that the Hungarians have made famous. The museum displays hoes, rakes, and other implements used in cultivating the fruit. Its curators enjoy telling about the types of peppers and how they are grown. Paprika is the main crop in the fertile district between Kalocsa and Szeged. Thousands of acres of the plants stretch as far as one can see.

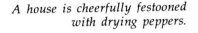

A house is cheerfully festooned with drying peppers.

The soil around Kalocsa is more conducive to the growing of very hot, light-colored peppers, and the land near Szeged is best for its brilliant red, but not so hot, paprika. After hand picking the peppers, harvesters hang them to dry from the rafters outside their houses.

October is a colorful time in southern Hungary, with all the buildings draped in clumps of crimson peppers. Once dried, the peppers are bagged and taken to the local cooperative for shipment to processing plants. It takes about 3 pounds (1.3 kilograms) of fruit to make 1 pound (.4 kilograms) of ground paprika.

Experienced pepper eaters in Kalocsa warn that the seeds should be removed before eating. Otherwise, the peppers are too spicy. Yet not all the peppers are *eros*, or hot. Some are *edes*, sweet. They are added to soup, stew, salads, or are eaten raw.

Left: In Hajos the vineyards are guarded to keep birds away. Above: Each of these houses has a wine cellar.

HAJOS

Fifteen miles (twenty-four kilometers) from Kalocsa is Hajos, Hungary's famous cellar village. German settlers here are known for their wine-making skills. Each family has a cool, dank house or cellar that is used to make its special wine. The grapes are grown on the Hosszuhegy State Farm outside the town. The hospitable wine makers enjoy sharing samples with visitors. It is easy to become fairly tipsy by the time a guest makes it partway down the row of cellars.

ESZTERGOM

Slovakia is directly across the Danube from Esztergom in northern Hungary. The remains of a bridge lie in the water at the foot of both banks, another reminder of World War II. The bridge was never replaced, so motorists have to travel farther to the northwest before finding a border crossing.

Esztergom is situated on the Duna River.

The Esztergom cathedral, high on a bluff above the city, is the largest in Hungary. It is the administrative seat for the country's Roman Catholic church. The cardinal-primate, who is Hungary's chief religious authority, makes Esztergom his home.

Esztergom's Christian Museum is one of the most important in Hungary. It has many rare fourteenth- and fifteenth-century paintings in its extensive collection. The Catholic church operates the museum, which is subsidized by the government.

The city was once a Roman settlement and had been Hungary's capital at the beginning of the medieval era. In fact, St. Stephen was born and crowned king here. The Turks devastated the city,

Vineyards in the Esztergom area

using its buildings as storehouses and barracks. Today, everything is bright and fresh with flowers. A small carnival attracts customers in the city square. Eager youngsters cluster around a shooting gallery, popping away at a row of tin ducks.

The agony of the Hungarians was revenged on the nearby "Turkish Rock," which can be seen from the highway. The bony pinnacle, soaring above the plain, was the execution site for captured Ottomans. The Hungarians would tie their enemies to the backs of horses and chase them over the cliff to their deaths. Now a towering radio antenna crowns the rock.

This then is Hungary: a bit of history, some peppers, beautiful architecture, and culture.

In this small Hungarian village, each home has its own adjoining vegetable garden.

Chapter 6

HUNGARY'S
ECONOMIC SCENE

Hungary is one of the richest countries of Eastern Europe, due to its strong blend of industry, agriculture, and tourism. Until 1989 the Soviet Union was a major trading partner, accounting for at least 35 percent of Hungary's exports. The railroad junction at Zahony in northeastern Hungary was always busy with the rattling of freight cars back and forth between the two nations. However, Hungary successfully extended its economic contacts with the rest of the world as well. Foreign buyers appreciate Hungarian craftsmanship and attention to detail.

In turn, this creates a favorable trade balance. Approximately five million Hungarians were active workers during the mid-1980s. The government allowed workers to join their local Economic Work Association, where they can hire out to other factories after regular hours. Workers and industry both benefit under the plan, as workers earn more and manufacturing plants keep up with production quotas. However, late 1980s world recession slowed Hungary's progress.

Tourists enjoying a wagon ride on the puszta (left) and strolling along a quaint old street in a northern suburb of Budapest (right)

TOURISM

Health care and schooling are free. Although inflation is driving prices up for Hungarians, living expenses in Hungary are generally lower than in many other nations, which makes Hungary an attractive tourist destination. Lush scenery, inexpensive room rates, and gracious hosts attract about twenty million tourists a year. Today's guests bring much-needed foreign currency into the country, which helps Hungary purchase raw materials and goods from abroad. The largest number of Eastern European tourists come from Slovakia, Hungary's northern neighbor. Hungary is preparing to hold a world's fair in 1996. Many tourists from all over the world are expected to visit the exposition.

To accommodate the flood of visitors, camps, hotels, and other vacation facilities are being constructed everywhere. Helping the rush of guests find the best vacation tour or resort is IBUSZ, the largest tour company in Hungary. IBUSZ began operating in 1902 and coordinates trips for thousands of persons each year. Many come for a specific reason, such as horseback riding in Bugac or pheasant hunting near Lake Balaton.

PROTECTING NATURAL RESOURCES

The National Office for the Protection of Nature and Environment is responsible for preserving the natural resources of Hungary. About 5 percent of the land is set aside for national parkland to protect the plants and animals there. Hungary has improved water quality in vacation areas. The nation realizes that without this protection, these valuable resources will be lost forever.

Yet mistakes are sometimes made. There were no provisions to clear the old Danube riverbed after the water was diverted to a new hydroelectric power dam 35 miles (56 kilometers) north of Budapest. Environmentalists in Hungary protested the joint Hungarian-Czechoslovakian venture, which had been funded by Austrian banks. They formed a group called the Danube Circle and petitioned the government to make a more detailed study of the impact of the dam. They were afraid the Danube would become more polluted. In May 1989, work was suspended on the dam and in November the project was abandoned.

INDUSTRY

More than one hundred years ago, the great Hungarian statesman Lajos Kossuth said that a "nation without industry is a one-armed giant." Industrial growth increased in Hungary after World War II, switching the country from agriculture to manufacturing. In fact, about twenty years after the war,

The Esztergom Works, a heavy machine tool plant

industrial production was already ten times that of the prewar amount. Before the war, 50 percent of all industry was concentrated in Budapest. Today, it has spread around the country. But the increase in heavy industry meant that fewer consumer goods were produced. It also led to ecological damage.

When the Communists ruled, the means of production, the factories, and the transport of goods were mainly controlled by the government. This was necessary to provide for the smooth running of the state, according to Communist economic theory.

However, a growing independence appeared within the rigid system. Firms were given more responsibility in determining how much to produce and were responsible for assuring quality of the products they produced. As exports rose, centralized planning had to bend to accommodate the demands of the international marketplace.

Janos Kadar called this the New Economic Mechanism when he initiated the plan in 1968. Small businesses were encouraged and farmers could sell their own crops. This helped the Hungarians

A cement factory

attain an economic status higher than that of most of Eastern Europe.

However, problems developed in the late 1980s as Hungarian exports ran into competition from cheaper goods made in the Far East. In addition, many of the country's industrial plants were outmoded. Workers began to worry more as they saw higher prices and a decline in their standard of living. These problems helped defeat the Communist system in the 1990 elections.

Recently, foreign companies have begun to set up businesses in Hungary. The United States has invested about $650 million, more than any other nation. Chemical production is a major industry, one almost unheard of before World War II. Today, more than 100,000 persons in this field make artificial fertilizer, chemical fibers, truck tires, plastics, and pharmaceutical drugs. Towns such as Kazincbarcika, Szolnok, and Pet were just sleepy crossroads until chemical plants were built there.

Hungary does not manufacture automobiles, but supplies thousands of individual parts to companies in other countries. Hungary is also one of the world's leading producers of buses. Of one recent order of 12,034 vehicles, 11,081 were manufactured for export. Ikarus, motor coaches made with technical assistance from Volvo of Sweden, are seen throughout Europe. Some have even been purchased by municipal bus companies in the United States. Semitrailer trucks, cement haulers, cranes, and ships also are built in Hungary. Budapest's Ganz-Mavag factory makes train coaches and engines.

Hungary's manufacturing scene is very diverse. Its factories churn out radios, television sets, hair dryers, washing machines, spin dryers, gas and electric ranges, and computers. More than 400 million light bulbs are made in Hungary each year, many of which are exported.

Sometimes domestic companies can't keep up with the demand for a product. For instance, Hungarian plants make almost 300,000 bicycles a year. Yet each year about 200,000 more cycles must be imported. In addition, several hundred thousand tons of Hungarian alumina (used in aluminum production) must be smelted elsewhere because Hungary cannot produce enough cheap electricity for the job. Finished aluminum is then returned to Hungary for use in other products.

MINERAL DEPOSITS

There are few extensive mineral deposits. Only copper, lead, zinc, and a little iron are found in quantities sufficient for mining. But black coal and uranium ore are mined around Mecsek in southern Hungary. Natural gas and crude oil have recently been discovered in several locations on the plains. Yet Hungary must still import more than 20 percent of its energy sources, whether electrical power or raw fuel.

On the other hand, Hungary has most of Europe's bauxite deposits, and annually mines more than three million tons of the claylike ore. Bauxite forms the base for aluminum production, a major Hungarian industry.

Since Hungary lacks much mineral wealth, it often exchanges goods for raw materials. Hungary imports iron ore and coke and then makes rolled steel from these resources. The steel can subsequently be exported for sale or traded for more materials. Hungary also imports oil. The glow from the exhaust chimneys of giant refineries such as the one at Szazhalombatta light the dark Hungarian nights. Finished oil products are exported.

ATOMIC POWER

While most of Hungary's plants are powered by water-produced electricity or fossil fuels such as coal or oil, the nation's first atomic power plant went into operation in 1982 at Paks. The plant is actually a joint project between several nations. The Soviet Union provided the designs, some of the equipment, and consultants for the project. The reactor was made in Czechoslovakia. Special transport vehicles were made in Bulgaria and the German Democratic Republic. Poland made heat exchangers and sent one thousand laborers to help with construction.

By 1985, the plant was producing 15 percent of the country's

Farm workers (left) on their lunch break and a woman proudly displaying her radishes (right)

total electric power supply. This has saved millions of tons of oil, which could then be made into diesel fuel, gasoline, and other products. To conserve energy by other means, the resourceful Hungarians use their many thermal springs to heat greenhouses and burn corncobs to dry grain.

AGRICULTURE

Although manufacturing has taken the spotlight in the Hungarian economic scene, agriculture remains important. In addition to paprika and sweet peppers, Hungarian farms produce sunflower seeds, fruits, potatoes, sugar beets, grain, and livestock. Out of Hungary's total area of 23 million acres (9.3 million hectares), about 15.3 million (6 hectares) can be farmed. Fifty percent of that is used as cropland, 4 percent are orchards, 3 percent are vineyards, and the remainder is pasture and forest.

Hungary is famous for its spicy sausages, producing five

A worker in a salami factory (left) and ripe grapes being picked in the Tokaj area (right)

thousand tons for export annually. Hungarian-made Pick salami is made in Szeged and is very popular in the United States. The salami is served on thinly sliced rye or pumpernickel bread with sweet butter and green or red peppers. TERIMPEX, a government agency, oversees production of meat products.

Thousands of gallons of Hungarian wine are made each year. The wines from Lake Balaton and Mor are among the most famous. There are many stories about Hungarian wine. The deep red wine made in Eger is called *Egri Bikaver* (Bull's Blood). One tale says that the women of Eger brought pitchers of the wine to their men defending the walls of the city from attacking Turks. Supposedly, when the Turks heard that the Hungarians were drinking ''bull's blood,'' they ran away in fear. The wine from Tokaj is very sweet.

Hungarian people also enjoy soft drinks and Coca-Cola has bottling plants in seven Hungarian towns to satisfy the growing demand.

Left: Harvesting on a collective farm   Right: An indoor market in Budapest

Agriculture has always been a mainstay of Hungary. In the old days, estates owned by wealthy nobles kept most of the products for their own use or resale. The peasants had to make do with what was left over. When the Communists came to power after World War II, every farm of more than 148 acres (60 hectares) was divided up. However, the individual farmers did not have enough tractors, tools, or seed to take care of the rapid need for more food. In the late 1940s, many of the smaller farms were incorporated into state-run facilities, and others were made into cooperatives. In a cooperative, a group of farmers share the work and the profits. Goods are usually stored in a central warehouse.

Under the Communists, 27 percent of the farmland was state farms. Sixty-nine percent was held by cooperatives. Four percent was privately owned by people who worked at other jobs. Farmers could sell their own produce and village market day was always busy. By the 1990s most state and collective farms were broken up and replaced by individual farm ownership.

Budapest's Great Market near Liberty Bridge is always an exciting place. Barrels of sour cabbage, mounds of garlic, racks of

*Left: An old coal-burning steam
locomotive takes railway buffs for a ride.
Right: Handcrafted baskets for
sale in a farmers market*

pine funeral wreaths, stacks of handwoven baskets, piles of red
and black embroidered blouses, shelves of potted geraniums, and
cartons of fresh country eggs fill row upon row of stalls. The aisles
are packed with city residents mixing with the country folk.
Everybody is bargaining, pinching, looking, and filling shopping
bags. On the sidewalks outside are vendors selling blue jeans,
razor blades, running shorts, and tennis shoes.

TRANSPORTATION

The geographical position of Hungary means that it is still a
crossroads nation. The country has more than 4,734 miles (7,619
kilometers) of railroads, much of it electrified. The first Hungarian
railway was built in 1846, chugging along with Belgium-made
engines between Pest and Vac. Today, tourists can see many old-
fashioned steam trains at a museum near Nagycenk, at the former
estate of Count Istvan Szechenyi. The count was a strong advocate
of railroads and loved riding them.

Besides the subway in Budapest, other forms of transportation include an expressway that goes to the northeast (left) and up-to-date buses and trams (right).

An extensive network of roads binds all corners of Hungary. About 18,600 miles (29,934 kilometers) of paved highway weave across the landscape to accommodate the more than 800,000 private autos in the country. The cars are imported from many countries.

It takes about a year's wages for a factory worker to buy a car. But everyone wants to own one.

For those who don't own cars, public transportation is what they must use. Trolleys, buses, and subways are available and heavily used every day.

Excellent waterways throughout Hungary allow the shipment of goods. A new system of locks and dams is being constructed on the lower Danube. This will make Belgrade, Yugoslavia, accessible to ships that pass through Budapest.

Three large locks, which control the level of water, have been built on the Tisza River. The most recent lock was opened in 1985 at Csongrad, finally connecting the entire eastern part of Hungary with the Danube via canals.

Hungarian air transportation dates back to the middle of the twentieth century. Tiny hydroplanes, taking off from the Danube, used to ferry mail and some brave passengers from Budapest to Vienna and Belgrade.

Now, the Hungarian airline Malev serves dozens of cities in Europe, the Middle East, and East Africa. It also flies to New York's Kennedy Airport. Budapest's Ferihegy International Airport bustles with traffic, accommodating Malev and flights from other international carriers. The departure terminal for international flights is always a bedlam of bags, shouts, and scurrying people. A popular site in the building is a tiny gift shop near the entrance where last-minute purchases of crafts, wine, magazines, and newspapers are made.

ECONOMIC OUTLOOK

Hungary is certainly making long strides in its quest to improve living conditions for its people. Czech crystal, French perfumes, and other imported, expensive items can still be purchased by wealthier Hungarians. Yet troublesome economic difficulties still cloud the horizon. Older pensioners often have difficulty matching fixed incomes with rising prices. Younger people take two or three jobs to keep up. But economists are planning how to utilize Hungary's strengths to preserve what is good. Moving from a rigidly controlled economic system to an open market and world economic problems caused Hungary's government to adopt austerity measures to control its foreign debt by the 1990s. It will not be easy to resolve current economic problems.

The Houses of Parliment in Budapest overlook the Danube. Janos Kadar (inset) was the first secretary of the Communist party.

Chapter 7

FROM POLITICS
TO RESEARCH

GOVERNMENT

Hungary is a republic. It has a president and a premier. The premier is the head of the National Assembly, which is the Hungarian legislature.

In 1989, Hungary declared its independence from the Soviet Bloc. In March and April 1990, free elections were held. For the first time in more than forty years, Hungarians could vote for candidates from more than one party. A new democratic government, consisting of many political parties, took office in May 1990.

The leading party in the new government is the Hungarian Democratic Forum. Together with its allied parties, the Independent Smallholders' party and the Christian Democratic People's party, it controls about 60 percent of the members of the National Assembly.

The premier of the new government is Jozsef Antal. The most important rival parties in the National Assembly are the Federation of Free Democrats and the Hungarian Socialist party.

The government's program emphasizes personal and political freedom and human rights.

THE NATIONAL ASSEMBLY

The National Assembly, or Parliament, enacts laws and makes the day-to-day decisions that run the country. The Assembly meets in a magnificent hall in Budapest, fronting the Danube. The Parliament Building looks like a giant rectangular gingerbread house with its ornate facade, central dome, and many spires. When construction was finally finished in 1904, the building was considered one of the largest structures in the world, covering more than 49,500 square feet (4,606 square meters). There is always a lot of ceremony when the Assembly begins a session there. The Assembly meets four times a year to discuss the budget, consider government policy, hear reports, and perform its other duties.

Members of the National Assembly are elected to a five-year term by eligible voters. Hungarians can vote when they reach eighteen, and are usually quite conscientious about going to the polls. They take their citizenship rights very seriously. There are 386 members in the National Assembly—about one member for every thousand voters.

A twenty-one-member Presidential Council elected by the Assembly exercises power when the Assembly is not in session. The council ratifies treaties, calls legislative sessions, and appoints judges, among its many other duties. The council is still directly responsible to Parliament, however, which reviews its activities during regular Assembly sessions.

THE COUNCIL OF MINISTERS

The administrative branch of the Hungarian government is the

Council of Ministers, headed by a prime minister. The prime minister is one of the most powerful officers in the government. The council corresponds to the presidential cabinet in the United States. Ministers are responsible for foreign trade, communications, finance, justice, industry, interior affairs, defense, health, agriculture, and similar functions. The council meets regularly to discuss topics ranging from consumer prices to energy consumption. The sessions help each minister know what the others are doing.

THE JUDICIARY

The judicial branch of the Hungarian government ensures that legislation conforms to the constitution. There are two independent branches of the judiciary: the courts and the prosecutors. The Hungarian Supreme Court has the final word on major legal matters. City and district courts act much as the lower courts do in the United States. The prosecutors, part of the Attorney General's office, are important judiciary personnel. In addition to supervising ordinary police operations regarding crime, the prosecutors check on the activities of individuals, social groups, and state agencies. Their power is very broad, extending throughout all levels of Hungarian society.

POLITICAL AND SOCIAL ORGANIZATIONS

Hungarians belong to many political and social organizations. Before 1990, the only political party with any influence was the Hungarian Socialist Workers party (HSWP), which was the Communist party. Any Hungarian who wished to have a job in the government had to belong to the HSWP.

In 1989, the HSWP changed its name to the Hungarian Socialist party (HSP). The HSP tried to hold on to its power by allowing reforms in the government. Other political parties were allowed to form and take part in government. But when elections were held in March and April 1990, the HSP was defeated. It received only 8.5 percent of the votes.

However, by 1994 parliamentary elections, many Hungarians had become disenchanted with the problems caused by transition to a free market system. The Socialist party won a majority, 209 of the 385 seats, and can thus form its own government. Gyula Horn, the Socialist leader and most likely next prime minister, said that his party would seek a coalition government with the Alliance of Free Democrats party which won the remaining seats.

The union movement in Hungary dates back more than one hundred years. Powerful printers, cobblers, and other craft unions were most active in Pest, even before that community merged with Buda. Many of the unions objected to Hungarian involvement in World War I and led numerous strikes, hoping to get the country out of war.

They were active in supporting Bela Kun's Communist government, and were greatly restricted following the downfall of his government. After World War II, the Communist unions edged out the independent trade groups and were leaders in the formation of the postwar system of government.

Young people were encouraged to join the Hungarian Communist Youth Organization, also known as the Communist Youth Federation. In addition to organizing sports and cultural programs, the representatives of the youth group were active in politics. They also help with harvests and assist in factories,

A conductor on the Youth Railway

perhaps working in plant nurseries and cafeterias. Membership in the federation was usually a stepping stone into the HSWP and a good career.

Within the umbrella youth union is the Union of Hungarian Pioneers, a copy of an organization of the same name in the Soviet republics, similar to scouts. Unofficially called Young Pioneers, the members sport bright red scarves tied around their necks. More than a million elementary school pupils belong. Hungarian youngsters think it is great fun to join the Pioneers. They go camping and sailing, learn crafts, and attend parties and outings. Best of all, the Pioneers get to operate the Youth Railway in Budapest.

Before joining the Pioneers, Hungarian youngsters can belong to the Young Drummers when they are six years old. At seven, there is an impressive initiation ceremony into the regular Pioneers.

There are many other social organizations in Hungary, including the Patriotic People's Front, the National Peace Council, the National Council of Hungarian Women, and the World Federation of Hungarians. The World Federation held an international meeting in Budapest in 1985, attracting thousands of Hungarians who now live elsewhere in the world. A folk festival was the highlight of the program. All these organizations are considered official arms of the state, and they promote the major aims of the government.

Hungarians are very world conscious. They belong to the United Nations and other international groups. Many associations have found that Hungary's centralized location makes it convenient for meetings. One of the largest international sessions held recently in Hungary was the 7th Congress of the Lutheran World Federation, based in Geneva, Switzerland. More than one thousand delegates met in Budapest in 1984.

There was some hesitancy at first on the part of the Lutherans to meet in Hungary. They remembered the imprisonment of their Bishop Lajos Ordas in the early days of the Communist regime. But the program was successful and the Lutherans were warmly greeted. Since the 1960s, the state and church have agreed to co-exist in Hungary. It was agreed that both camps could work together for the betterment of the nation and that belief in God was not a detriment to being a patriotic Hungarian. The constitution also ensures the free practice of religion. In fact, many Hungarians of all ages are still regular churchgoers. In 1988 the government began to work more closely with the church. The government called for the church to work with it to help solve the country's problems. The government allowed religious schools to be formed and permitted the celebration of St. Stephen's Day.

Children from a day-care facility being taken on a walk

HEALTH AND SOCIAL WELFARE

The average life expectancy of Hungarian men is around sixty-six years of age. For women, it's about seventy-four. People are living longer as Hungary becomes more industrially developed and as economic wealth increases. However, problems have accompanied the benefits. Heart and circulatory diseases have increased, possibly due to the stress of living in a fast-paced technological world.

Yet, infant mortality is down and the birthrate has increased. The children of working mothers are cared for in nurseries and day boarding schools if they are too young to attend school. A working mother can stay at home and draw sick pay if her baby is ill. She can also remain at home for up to three years, if she wants to look after her toddler before returning to work. Families receive allowances from the government, depending on the number of children they have. There are also more supplements for retarded youngsters and for families with more than two children. The government believes these allotments raise the living standards.

Health care and hospitalization are free in Hungary. Tending for the sick are about 33 thousand doctors. Many of them are women who have found that being a physician is a rewarding career. In addition to helping the ill, Hungarian hospitals and institutes conduct research into finding cures for diseases.

The Cardiological Institute, the Research Institute of Medical Sciences, and the Semmelweis University of Medical Sciences in Budapest are highly respected worldwide for their work.

A sick worker can spend as much time as needed in a hospital and receive sick pay as high as 75 percent of regular salary.

The pension system covers everyone, from laborers to professional people. More than two million retired or handicapped Hungarians are now on pensions. Since they have worked for the benefit of Hungary for many years, it is felt that the workers should receive help in their old age. There are more than 250 nursing homes for the elderly, accommodating over 30,000 clients. Day programs provide meals for senior citizens who are healthy enough to remain in their own homes. Social workers help with shopping, laundry, and similar household tasks.

EDUCATION

Hungary has one of the highest literacy rates in Europe. Since more children are being born, Hungary is working to keep up with the demand for classrooms. Youngsters must attend school until they are sixteen years old. After elementary school they can attend a gymnasium, which offers college preparatory courses.

A primary school class at work

Other youngsters enroll in a technical school to learn a trade. More than a quarter of a million young people attend one or the other of these types of institutions. Some 107 thousand students attend Hungarian universities. The love of learning is strong in Hungary. Another forty thousand people take correspondence courses or go to night school after a full workday.

Adult summer school is usually popular, especially when courses include folk art, cinematography, or wild game management. The programs are held at the universities in Pecs, Szeged, Budapest, Kecskemet, Sopron, and elsewhere.

Languages are popular requirements in Hungarian schools. Most children speak several tongues without much difficulty. Of course, in a typical school, each pupil must take Hungarian language classes. Two years of English, one year of French, and one year of German are also taught. Children study literature, mathematics, geography, history, biology, art, gymnastics, and music. By the time a youngster is in the sixth school year, he or she is taking some chemistry and physics.

At Budapest University, a professor gives a lecture.

The feminist movement is very strong in Hungary, since many professional and government workers are women. In 1988, a woman, Ilona Tatai, was appointed to the Politburo, the highest government council. She was the manager of the Taurus Rubber Works. Yet girls are still often slotted into traditional home economics courses such as sewing. Boys, however, are taught metal and woodworking.

A typical Hungarian school offers many after-hour activities. Literature, library, physics, folk dancing, target shooting, and other clubs are popular. Older children tutor the younger ones, helping them with spelling, writing, and speaking. Parents are urged to become involved in school programs and escort students on field trips, talk to classes about their professions, help out in the lunchrooms, and organize parties.

SCHOLARS AND INVENTORS

Over the centuries, Hungarian scholars have made important contributions to numerous disciplines. They evolved out of a long tradition, as evidenced by the fact that the first university in Hungary was founded at Pecs in 1367.

Explorer-linguist Sandor Korosi Csoma wrote the first English-Tibetan dictionary early in the nineteenth century. Lorand Eotvos invented a special pendulum still used by researchers looking for oil. Donat Banki and Janos Csonka produced the first working carburetor, now a requirement for any automobile engine. University of Szeged Professor Albert Szent-Gyorgyi received the 1937 Nobel Prize for medicine. He worked with the Vitamin C properties of peppers. Noteworthy mathematicians have included Gyorgy Alexits, Laszlo Redei, and Alfred Renyi. Notable Hungarian chemists have been Tibor Erdey-Gruz, Elemer Schulek, and Jozsef Varga.

Many of these personalities were members of the Hungarian Academy of Sciences, founded in 1825. The academy promotes international meetings on numerous subjects, publishes books, and encourages research in many fields. The Agricultural Research Institute of the academy developed many techniques for quality plant breeding. It works in a magnificent chateau at Martonvasar, often visited by brilliant composer Ludwig van Beethoven in the 1800s. Automatic equipment in forty-four different chambers can simulate any sort of growing condition needed to study a particular plant cycle.

The academy runs dozens of other research facilities, including the Institute of Astronomy, the Central Physics Research Institute, and the Telecommunications Research Institute.

Hungarians have always been eager to accept a challenge. Yet they haven't lost their sense of humor. The mind-twisting, multicolored puzzle called the Rubik's Cube was designed by Erno Rubik.

A professional ballet troupe performing at the Budapest Opera House (above)
and German-Hungarian folk dancing (below) in Hajos

Chapter 8

VIBRANT ARTS,
ACTIVE SOCIETY

Hungary's cultural offerings are a resplendent rainbow. Lively foot-tapping dances, delicately imaginative artwork, and introspective literature blend easily with wonderful folk traditions.

LITERATURE

Since the first clerks toiled in St. Stephen's court, writers have been respected by Hungarians. Their literature has the zest of paprika. The country's authors pack a wallop and have often gotten in trouble for it. They have died in revolutions, were jailed for their beliefs, and have been tortured by their enemies. The honor roll is long, including such names as poet Balint Balassi, who was killed fighting the Turks. Careers often crossed from the professional to the artistic and back again. Miklos Zrinyi was a noted author, as well as a brilliant soldier and able politician.

Poet Sandor Petofi was killed by the Russians on a Transylvania battlefield. He was one of thousands of slain freedom fighters in the Hungarian War for Independence. His battered body was dumped into an unmarked grave, a tragic ending for a brilliant young writer. To cheer his fellow soldiers, Petofi, son of a tavern keeper, had written many verses about the Hungarian puszta, where he was born.

Another poet, Dezso Koztolanyi, was saddened by the turmoil. Yet he was still able to see beyond the unhappiness. His second volume of poetry, *A Szegeny Kisgyermek Panaszai* (Complaints of a Poor Little Child), is a generally lighthearted peek back at his adolescence.

Koztolanyi magically writes about his dreams and disappointments. He tells stories about the family doctor, his grandfather, and pals from school. Koztolanyi touched on everyday life. One of his best-loved poems is the delicate *Lanc, Lanc, Eszterlanc* ("Twine, Twine, Intertwine").

It is estimated that an average of nine books a year are purchased by Hungarian readers, who devour the latest novels as well as literary classics. Book Week is always a popular spring feature in Budapest, traditionally the time when publishers release their new works.

Hungary can boast of more than five thousand publicly owned libraries and more than four thousand run by trade unions and social organizations. Special children's sections are well utilized. Youngsters curl up on rugs or snuggle into comfortable chairs for a quiet reading time.

Under the Communist government, there was no official censorship, but writers were expected to police themselves. This was difficult because it was hard to know what might be accepted or rejected by the government. No one was allowed to question or

A statue of Mihaly Vorosmarty, Hungarian poet and dramatist

criticize the Soviet presence in Eastern Europe. Complaining of Soviet policy in general and that of neighboring Communist states was also off-limits.

This does not mean that the Hungarians were afraid to publish anything critical. Not at all. There were several underground reviews, called *samizdat* (which means "self-publishing" in Russian), that printed stories that the government officially opposed.

Beszelo and *Dunataj* were two of the better-known magazines that published articles on social and political problems in Hungary. They ran pieces highlighting discrimination against Hungarians living in neighboring countries.

Although the circulation of these publications was limited, they were eagerly read by intellectuals and others who wanted to know what was really going on behind the scenes. Even the government bureaucrats snapped up copies. The Communists generally left samizdat alone.

THEATER AND FILM

Hungarian theater is known worldwide for colorful richness and stagecraft. Budapest has twenty-two major theaters offering full seasons, which typically begin in September and run through early July of the following year. Open-air theaters are popular in the summer. The National Theater Rally is annually held in late May or early June in Budapest, offering some of the best works of Hungarian and international playwrights. Szeged's open-air theater on Cathedral Square has excellently staged productions as well. Other fine regional theaters are found in Pecs, Kaposvar, and Zalaegerszeg. It is estimated that six million Hungarians attend the theater each year.

Most of the theater companies in Budapest were founded around the end of the nineteenth century. The Vigszinhaz (Comedy Theater) was established in 1896. The Kiraly Szinhaz (Theatre Royal) is home for operetta.

Several others stage cabaret shows or musical comedies. The magnificent Hungarian State Opera and the National Theater have their own halls, rebuilt after World War II. Since 1952, the State Village Theatre has toured the provinces, visiting villages that have no local company.

Famous contemporary directors include Mor Ditroi, Daniel Job, Otto Adam, Laszlo Vamos, and Endre Marton. Hungarian plays have been well received even outside the country. Performances of Istvan Orkeny's *The Tot Family* and Karoly Szakonyi's *Break in Transmission* have packed theaters in many nations.

In addition, Hungarians are eager film goers. They like locally produced movies and those produced outside the country. In fact, more than four hundred foreign films are dubbed into Hungarian each year. Hungary has over fifteen hundred cinemas, ranging from huge, gilt-edged buildings in the capital to smaller regional houses. Moviemaking has long been important on the cultural scene. The first Hungarian film was a newsreel shot in 1901 in Budapest. Twenty-five Hungarian movies were made in 1915. Of course those were silent films, but they were considered among the best made in Europe at the time. The Hungarian Film Company today produces about twenty full-length features and five hundred short films a year.

Some of today's movies focus on the horrors of World War II. Those terrible days are readily remembered. One of the most famous Hungarian films is *Somewhere in Europe*. Made in 1947, it tells of children made homeless by the war.

Many other films are documentaries, such as Imre Gyongyossy's look at Hungarian gypsy culture in *You're Stark Naked*. Some of Sandor Petofi's famous poetic characters have been made into cartoons by Marcell Jankovich.

Today's filmmakers tackle all sorts of subjects. Gyorgy Szomjas produced *The Wall Driller* in 1985, which told about a bored young Hungarian who bought a power drill and rented out his hole-drilling services to neighbors. Geza Bremenyi's *Great Generation* took place in a Budapest disco, the Elvis Presley Club.

PAINTING, SCULPTURE, AND CRAFTS

Painting, sculpture, and crafts are popular as well. The Hungarian National Gallery in Buda Castle annually features major exhibitions of local artists. In 1983, the largest and most comprehensive show of contemporary Hungarian craftwork was displayed, including six hundred pieces by 154 artists.

The National Art Gallery in Budapest

Thousands of art fans pour into such shows to compare, comment, and criticize. There are at least 23,000 amateur art groups in Hungary, with some 500,000 members.

MUSEUMS

Hungary is a nation of museums, with 550 facilities containing 8.8 million artifacts, ranging from stamps to farm equipment. October is celebrated as Museum Month, with each museum offering special shows. Twenty-two museums are in Budapest. One of the most important is the National Museum, where schoolchildren gaze in awe at exhibits covering their country's thousand-year history. Complete villages, such as a museum complex at Zalaegerszeg, have been restored to the way they looked centuries ago. The whitewashed houses are roofed with rushes. The rooms are full of period furniture.

MUSIC AND MUSICIANS

The sweeping strains of Hungarian music have greatly influenced composers around the world. Franz Liszt was noted for

Statues of two famous Hungarian composers and musicians: Bela Bartok (far left) and Franz Liszt

his rich, romantic composition. Composer Bela Bartok and educator Zoltan Kodaly remain at the pinnacle of the international musical world, followed closely by contemporaries Attila Bozay, Janos Decsenyi, Zsolt Durko, and numerous others.

Sandor Szokolay is one of the most productive of today's new wave of musicians. He has written three full-length operas and numerous works for choirs and orchestras. One of his major works was translated into nine languages.

New talent is constantly appearing. Zoltan Kocsis won numerous international piano competitions as a youngster. In 1973, when he was only twenty-one, he was appointed a professor at the National Academy of Music.

Folk music remains popular. The Hungarian State Folk Ensemble has appeared in more than thirty countries, demonstrating national dances and songs.

The Hungarian recording company, Hungarotoon, has been a major European producer, pressing millions of discs each

Hungarian gypsies, who make up about 3 percent of the population, keep their own customs and speak a dialect called Romany.

year, including special releases marking anniversaries, such as Brahms' birthday. The rock opera *Stephan and the King* by Levente Szorenyi, with lyrics by Janos Brody, has been a gold album seller throughout Europe.

Every Hungarian restaurant worthy of the name has a gypsy orchestra. The wild strains are a perfect counterpoint to any meal, whether spooning up chunks of peppery fish soup called *ponty-halazzle* in a laborers' restaurant or gourmet dining on a huge dessert plate of *makos teszta*, made of noodles, poppy seeds, and sugar.

An orchestra usually consists of a clarinet, two fiddles, a bass, and cimbalon. The latter instrument is similar to a dulcimer, but is played with a smaller hammer. The music is handed down from father to son by these dark-skinned, proud people. Sandor Lakatos, one of the most famous gypsy band leaders, gave a concert tour of the United States in 1984.

Hungarian gypsies comprise about 3 percent of the total population. Originally, they were a nomadic people from India, and they still prefer living apart from the rest of the Magyar population. The gypsies have kept their own customs and speak a dialect called Romany.

Above: Gypsies entertain patrons at a restaurant in Budapest. Below:
Delicious entrées (left) and hearty breads (right) are attractively presented.

SPORTS

Hungarians are keenly interested in sports. Their accomplishments in archery, boxing, and motorcycle racing have shattered worldwide records. At the first modern Olympic games in Athens in 1896, the Hungarian athletes there won two first places, one second, two thirds, and one fourth. In addition, Dr. Ferenc Kemeny, a teacher from Eger, was one of the founding members of the International Olympic Committee.

International tourneys in ice hockey, gymnastics, and similar events utilize Budapest's huge Sports Hall or the ninety-thousand-seat People's Stadium.

Hungary has always fielded strong swimmers, starting with architect Alfred Hajos, who won the 100-meter and 1,200-meter swim meets at those first Olympics. Sandor Wladar won a gold medal in the backstroke at the 1980 Moscow Olympics. Alban Vermes took second place in the 200-meter breaststroke in the 1983 European Championships in Rome. The Hungarian water polo team, coached by Peter Rusoran, also won a second place in those hard-fought championships.

Swimming is a popular sport in schools and is usually a part of the physical education program. Most new schools are being built with enclosed pools for year-round use.

Canoeing and kayak racing are also competitive sports in Hungary. The Danube provides training challenges that are met by Hungarian rowers like Geza Csapo, who won three gold medals in the 1973 world championships in Tampere, Finland.

Football, or soccer, is played everywhere in Hungary. More than 100,000 players are registered. The Hungarian team in the 1950s was tagged the ''Mighty Magyars,'' because they seemed to

High school students out jogging

steamroll over their opponents. They even defeated such powerhouses as England, which had never been beaten before by a team from the European continent.

The 1986 national soccer team fought its way to the finals of the World Cup soccer championships in Mexico before being edged out of play in the preliminary games. One of their toughest opponents was the Soviet Union, which defeated the Hungarians, 6 to 0.

Athletics in Hungary are directed by the National Office for Physical Education and Sports, which is attached to the Council of Ministers. Local governing bodies are in every Hungarian town, helping coordinate training, arranging for fields and playing sites, and directing programs for youngsters. There are about 4,400 individual sporting clubs in Hungary, with almost two million members, for those interested in track and field, swimming, and other sports. Coaches are trained at the Hungarian Physical Training College.

In 1988 the World Figure Skating Championships were held in Budapest. Skaters from all over the world competed.

Hungarians enjoy occasions for celebrating, such as the
wine festival (above) and the wedding procession (below).

FESTIVALS

Hungarians still keep a keen eye turned on their past. After all, more than one thousand years of history can't be forgotten. Folk festivals abound. One of the most popular, now a tourist attraction, is the buso, a pre-Lenten procession at Mohacs. Grotesque masks are worn in the parades that wend their way around the city. In the days of the Turkish occupation, the masks were used to frighten evil spirits.

A fishing festival at Baja is complete with fireworks and a nighttime procession of lighted ships.

New Year's Eve balls in Budapest harken back to the days of the empire, with full orchestras, fancy dining, and plenty of dancing.

From the past through the present, Hungarians have remained an eager people. But in their rush toward the future, they have never forgotten their hospitality. This is typified by an adage that says a visitor arrives in Hungary as a guest and leaves as a friend. No one can argue with that.

MAP KEY

Abony	B5			
Adony	B4	Komlo	B4	
Bacsalmas	B4	Koppany River	B4	
Baja	B4	Kormend	B3	
Balaton Lake	B3, B4	Kunszentmarton	B5	
Balmazujvaros	B5	Lajosmizse	B4	
Bataszek	B4	Mako	B5	
Battonva	B5	Mateszalka	B6	
Békés	B5	Melykut	B4	
Bekescsaba	B5	Mezokovesd	B5	
Berettyoujfalu	B5	Mezotur	B5	
Bicske	B4	Miskolc	A5	
Bodva River	A5, B5	Mohacs	C4	
Budapest	B4	Monor	B4	
Cegled	B4	Mor	B4	
Csongard	B5	Mosonmagyarovav	B3	
Csorna	B3	Nagykanizsa	B3	
Danube River	B3, B4, C4	Nagykoros	B4	
Debrecen	B5	Nyiregyhaza	B5	
Derecske	B5	Oroshaza	B5	
Devavanya	B5	Ozd	A5	
Duna River	B4, C4	Paks	B4	
Dunafoldvar	B4	Papa	B3	
Dunapataj	B4	Pécs (Pecs)	B4	
Dunaujvaros	B4	Polgar	B5	
Eger	B5	Puspokladany	B5	
Ercsi	B4	Raba River	B3	
Erd	B4	Salgotarjan	A4	
Esztergom	B4	Sárbogárd	B4	
Gyongyos	B4	Sarospatak	A5	
Györ (Gyor)	B3	Sarvar	B3	
Gyula	B5	Satoraljaujhely	A5	
Hajduböszörmeny	B5	Siklos	C4	
Hajduhadhaz	B5	Sopron	B3	
Hajdunanas	B5	Sumeg	B3	
Hajduszoboszlo	B5	Szamos River	A6, B6	
Harnad River	A5	Szarvas	B5	
Hatvan	B4	Szeged	B5	
Heves	B5	Székesfehérvár	B4	
Hódmezövásárhely	B5	Szekszard	B4	
Ipoly River	B4	Szentendre	B4	
Janoshalma	B4	Szentes	B5	
Jaszapati	B5	Szigetvar	B3	
Jaszbereny	B4	Szolnok	B5	
Kalocsa	B4	Tata	B4	
Kaposvar	B3	Tatabánya (Tatabanya)	B4	
Kapuvár (Kapuvar)	B3	Tisza River	A5, A6, B5	
Karcag	B5	Tiszafured	B5	
Kazincbarcika	A5	Tokaj	A5	
Kecskemét (Kecskemet)	B4	Tolna	B4	
Keszthely	B3	Torokszentmiklós	B5	
Kiskoros	B4	Totkomlos	B5	
Kiskundorozsma	B5	Turkeve	B5	
Kiskunfelegyhaza	B4	Vac	B4	
Kiskunhalas	B4	Varpalota	B4	
Kiskunmajsa	B4	Vecses	B4	
Kisujszallas	B5	Veszprem	B3	
Kisvarda	A6	Veszto	B5	
Komádi	B5	Zala River	B3	
Komarom	B4	Zalaegerszeg	B3	

MINI-FACTS AT A GLANCE

GENERAL INFORMATION

Official Name: Magyar Nepkoztarsasag (Republic of Hungary)

Capital: Budapest

Official Language: Magyar (Hungarian)

Government: Hungary is a republic governed by a president, a premier, and the Hungarian parliament, the National Assembly. All legislation is nominally ratified by the National Assembly, whose 386 members are chosen by national elections. Major parties are the Hungarian Democratic Forum, the Independent Smallholders' party, and the Christian Democratic People's party. Together, these three parties control 60 percent of the seats in the National Assembly. Other important parties are the Federation of Free Democrats and the Hungarian Socialist party. Administrative functions are executed by the Council of Ministers, whose members are selected by the Presidential Council and approved by the National Assembly. Judicial authority rests with the Hungarian Supreme Court.

National Song: "Himnusz" ("Hymn")

Flag: Horizontal stripes of red, white, and green, which are the traditional national colors. It was adopted in 1957. The coat of arms consists of St. Stephen's crown at the top, a shield with the national colors, and a wreath of wheat.

Money: The basic unit is the forint. In 1994, one forint was worth $.0099 in U.S. currency.

Weights and Measures: Hungary uses the metric system.

Population: Estimated 1994 population: 10,375,000; 1980 census–10,709,463. Distribution 65 percent urban, 35 percent rural.

Major Cities

Budapest	2,115,000
Debrecen	220,000
Miskolc	208,000
Szeged	189,000
Pecs	183,000
Gyor	132,000

(Population based on 1989 estimate)

Religion: About two-thirds of the Hungarian people are Catholics; most of the rest are Protestants, and most of those are Reformed (Calvinist) and Lutheran. Catholics of the Byzantine Rite, Jews, and Unitarians also are worthy of mention.

GEOGRAPHY

Highest Point: Mount Kekes, 3,330 ft. (1,015 m) above sea level

Lowest Point: Near Szeged, 259 ft. (79 m) above sea level

Mountains: Most of Hungary is a flat plain, with the exception of low mountains in the northcentral and northeastern sections and to the north and south of Lake Balaton. West of the Danube are the Bakony and Vertes mountains. Along the far northern border with Slovakia are the Matra Mountains.

Rivers: The main river is the Danube, which crosses the hills of Central Hungary in a narrow, steep-sided, deep valley. The river is navigable in its entire Hungarian section. The Danube and its two most important Hungarian tributaries, the Raba and the Drava, are of Alpine origin, while the Tisza and its tributaries, which drain much of eastern Hungary, rise in the Carpathians.

Climate: Hungary has a moderately dry continental climate. The temperature ranges from a chilly 32 to 25° F. (0 to -4° C) in January to July temperatures of 64 to 73° F. (18 to 23° C). In the lowlands precipitation generally ranges from 20 to 24 in. (50.8 to 60.9 cm), rising to 24 to 31 in. (60.9 to 78.8 cm) over higher areas. May, June, and July are the wettest months.

Greatest Distances: East to west—312 mi. (502 km)
North to south—193 mi. (311 km)

Area: 35,919 sq. mi. (93,030 km²)

NATURE

Trees: The Transdanubian lands and the mountains are covered by deciduous woodland—oak, beech, lime, and chestnut—but in the area approaching the Great Plains, steppe conditions prevail. The Great Plains was once wooded like the rest of Hungary, but early invaders from Asia brought extensive flocks of grazing animals that prevented the reestablishment of tree cover. Reclamation projects have attempted to improve the land through irrigation and reforestation.

Animals: Boars are the largest wild animals of the mountain ranges and are found also on the hilly countrysides. There are hare, foxes, deer, wild pigs, wild cats, and some remnants of the once-abundant beaver and otter. Pulis, rough-coated dogs, keep watch on herds of cows, sheep, and swine.

Birds: Hungary is one of the most important stations for bird migration between northern Europe and Africa. Common birds are storks, cranes, and swallows, as well as herons, hawks, and plovers. Part of Lake Balaton is kept as a reservation for bird life, especially the swamp species. The heron is the most spectacular bird in this preserve, although other examples of marsh waterfowl also survive.

Fish: In this landlocked country, the carp is the predominant fish.

EVERYDAY LIFE

Food: Hungarians are lovers of good food, especially on special occasions. Soups are an important part of the diet. Goulash is a soup that resembles a stew and is generally made of cubes of meat with onions, potatoes, and gravy. It is usually flavored with paprika, Hungary's favorite spice.

Pork is the favorite meat, although poultry and beef are popular as well. The best-known Hungarian pastry is strudel, made from a flaky, thin crust usually filled with fruit or cheese. Hungarian wines are excellent.

Housing: The shortage of housing in Hungary is a result of the rapid shift from rural to urban areas, and it persists despite a number of government programs. Overcrowding and shared tenancy are common.

Rural families usually live in small stucco houses with tile roofs. The houses surround central courtyards, with only a window or two facing the sunny side of the street. Many are still without electricity. Urban dwellings tend to be large apartment complexes with small individual units.

Holidays:

January 1, New Year's Day
March 15, Anniversary of the 1848 Revolution
April 4, Liberation Day
May 1, Labor Day
August 20, St. Stephen's Day
December 25, Christmas Day
December 26, Boxing Day

Culture: Hungary in general, and especially Budapest, is noted for its vigorous and rich cultural life.

The democratic and progressive ideals of the nineteenth century developed an important current in Hungarian literature. It reached its peak in the poetry of Sandor Petofi, the national poet, as well as in that of Janos Arany and Mihaly Vorosmarty, and in the historical novels of Mor Jokai.

In the twentieth century critical realism was developed in the novels of Kalman Mikszath and lyrical symbolism in the poetry of Endre Ady. A new trend with Marxist undertones developed after World War I in the poetry of Attila Jozsef. Other important writings of the interwar years were the poetry and prose of Gyula Illyes, the regional novels of Aron Tamasi, and the social and historical dramas and critical essays of Laszlo Nemeth.

Under the Communist regime writing was limited to themes of "social realism," and authors who deviated from the party line were punished. In the 1960s, the government began to relax its controls on cultural life, and writers and other artists were given some degree of freedom of expression.

Two Hungarian playwrights are internationally famous: Imre Madach and Ferenc Molnar.

Hungarian theaters are known worldwide for richness and stagecraft. Hungarians are avid filmgoers.

Painting reached its zenith in the nineteenth-century era of romanticism. Painters such as Viktor Madarasz, Gertalan Szekely, and Mihaly Zichy raised Hungarian painting to a level it has not equaled since.

In the Communist period, graphics became the most advanced form of Hungarian fine art through the works of Jeno Barcsay and Bela Kondor.

Hungarian music in the nineteenth century is primarily associated with names of Franz Liszt and Ferenc Serkel, creator of the Hungarian national opera.

Music in the twentieth century is associated with the names of Bela Bartok and Zoltan Kodaly, based on their research in folk music. Sandor Szokolay is one of the most productive contemporary musicians. He has written three full-length operas and numerous choral and orchestral works.

There are three institutions devoted to maintaining high levels of musical performance: The Budapest Philharmonic Society, the Music Academy, and the State Opera House.

There are 550 museum facilities in Hungary, 22 of which are in Budapest.

Sports: Spectator sports are very popular, and the people participate in a variety of athletic activities. The government promotes sports with generous subsidies, and physical education is compulsory in the schools.

Soccer is the most popular sport, and there are more than 2,000 soccer fields and over 100,000 players. Other favorites are basketball, fencing, and volleyball. Swimming, boating, and fishing are popular also. Hungary has always had strong swimmers who have won many international competitions. Canoeing and kayak racing are competitive sports. Accomplishments in archery, boxing, and motorcycle racing have shattered worldwide records.

Communication: There are about 30 daily newspapers, which have a daily circulation of about 1,250,000 copies. The country has three radio and two television stations. The state owns and operates the radio and television network, as well as the telegraph, telephone, and postal services.

Transportation: Transport in Hungary is strongly centralized, and the main rail links and principal roads converge on Budapest. There is an upsurge in car ownership. Roads have overtaken railways in terms of the volume of freight transported. A majority of roads have modern asphalt or concrete surfaces. The London-Damascus and Hamburg-Bucharest international highways cross the country.

The Danube is the only waterway in the country transporting a significant amount of freight, most of it international. Tourism provides the bulk of a highly seasonal traffic on other waterways.

Because the country is so small, domestic air services are not economically feasible. International air traffic, however, is rapidly expanding. Malev, the national airline, flies to almost every country in Europe as well as to the United States and the Middle East.

Education: Hungary has one of the highest literacy rates in Europe. In Hungary schooling is free and compulsory between the ages of 6 and 16. Elementary education embraces the 6 to 14 age group. At the age of 14, children embark on their secondary education in college preparatory schools, technical schools, or schools specializing in fine arts or music. The curricula are laid down by the Ministry of Education and are standardized throughout the country. Technical schools have become increasingly popular. All schools, except for a few run by religious denominations, are operated by the state.

The first Hungarian university was founded at Pecs in 1367. There are more than 100 institutions of higher education ranging from the traditional university to the very specialized college, such as the College of Chemical Engineering at Kazincbarcika. Acceptance into universities is dependent on examinations.

Adult summer school programs are popular.

Health and Welfare: Medical treatment is available free of charge, as are most medicines and medical appliances. Medical care is generally of a high standard. Great attention is paid to disease prevention through screening for tuberculosis and cancer and immunization against smallpox, polio, and tuberculosis.

Social insurance, which is paid for by employers, provides for sickness, maternity, and death benefits. Mothers can receive a monthly grant for a period of three years after birth. Social and pension funds are administered by the Trade Union Social Insurance Center. Councils also provide homes for the aged for those who do not have immediate families.

ECONOMY AND INDUSTRY

Principal Products:

Agriculture: corn, potatoes, wheat, sugar beets, fruit, wine grapes, dairy products, livestock
Manufacturing: textiles, foods and beverages, aluminum, steel, chemicals, machinery, transportation equipment
Mining: bauxite

IMPORTANT DATES

Late 800s—Magyars conquer Hungary

955—Battle of Lechfeld; St. Adalbert converts some Magyars to Christianity

1000—Stephen I (later St. Stephen) becomes Hungary's first king and converts the country to Roman Catholicism

1222—King Andrew II signs Golden Bull establishing Parliament and limiting the king's power

1241—Mongols capture Hungary

1387—Sigismund of Luxembourg becomes king

1458-90—Matthias Corvinus rules Hungary; makes it a center of Italian Renaissance culture

1514—Peasants, led by Gyorgy Dozsa, revolt and are defeated

1526—Battle of Mohacs; the Ottoman Turks defeat Hungary and soon afterward occupy central and eastern Hungary

1686—Turks are driven from Budapest; Austrians take over

1703—Prince Rakoczi II leads an unsuccessful rebellion against the Austrians

1740—Maria Theresa of Austria becomes queen of Hungary

1848—Parliament drafts declaration of independence for Hungary

1849—Hungary is defeated by Austria's Franz Joseph

1867—Compromise of 1867 establishes dual monarchy of Austro-Hungary

1873—Budapest is formed from Buda, Obuda, and Pest

1914-18—Austro-Hungary is defeated in World War I

1918—Hungary becomes a republic; Count Mihaly Karolyi becomes prime minister

1919—First Hungarian Communist government is established by Bela Kun, but it does not last long; Rear Admiral Nicolas Horthy, a conservative, becomes regent of Hungary

1920—Treaty of Trianon, part of the peace settlement after World War I, takes away two-thirds of prewar Hungary

1941—Hungary enters World War II on the German side

1944—Germany occupies Hungary

1945—Hungary signs armistice with the Allies ending World War II

1946—Hungary again becomes a republic and institutes social and economic reforms

1946-49—Communists win control of the government; constitution is adopted

1955—Hungary joins the United Nations

1956—Soviet forces crush an anti-Communist uprising

1959—Janos Kadar becomes first secretary of the Communist Central Committee

1968—Government adopts New Economic Mechanism

1973—Hungary joins the General Agreement on Tariffs and Trade

1984—Seventh Congress of Lutheran World Federation meets in Hungary

1985—On March 20, the Congress of the Hungarian Socialist Workers party ended after reelecting Janos Kadar as party leader

1987—Karoly Nemeth is named president and Karoly Grosz prime minister

1988—Karoly Grosz succeeds Kadar as party leader; Miklos Nemeth succeeds Grosz as premier

1989—March 15 is observed as a new National Holiday honoring the 1848 Revolution Against Austrian Rule; the first independent trade union for blue collar workers is formed in Budapest

1990—In elections in March and April, the Hungarian Socialist party is voted out of power. A multiparty, democratic government takes office.

1994—Economic hardship brought on by government austerity measures to combat rising foreign debt, privatize state-owned business and adopt a free market system cause Hungarians to vote the Socialist (Communist) party back into parliamentary control

IMPORTANT PEOPLE

Endre Ady (1877-1919), considered greatest Hungarian lyric poet of the twentieth century

Almos (c. ninth century), first chief of the Seven Tribes, a federation of Magyars

Janos Arany (1817-82), poet

Arpad (d. 907), national hero of Hungary, founder of the Hungarian monarchy

Balint Balassa (1554-94), lyric poet

Bela Bartok (1881-1945), composer, leader of contemporary Hungarian music

Bela IV (1206-70), king of Hungary (1235-70); defeated in great Mongol invasion (1241)

Marcel Breuer (1902-81), Hungarian-born architect, director of the Bauhaus in Dessau, Germany (1925-28)

Ferenc Deak (1803-76), lawyer and statesman

Gyorgy Dozsa (1470-1514), rebel and soldier of fortune

Dennis Gabor (1900-79), Hungarian-born professor and physicist; inventor of the holograph for which he won the Nobel Prize in 1971

Karoly Grosz (1931-   ); becomes party leader in 1988

Theodor Herzl (1860-1904), writer and journalist; founder of Zionism

Gyorgy Hevesy (1885-1966), chemist, won the Nobel Prize for chemistry in 1943

Nicholas Horthy (1868-1957), rear admiral and statesman; regent of Hungary (1920-44)

Janos Hunyadi (1407?-1456), national hero of Hungary; leader against the Turks

Gyula Illyes (1902-   ), writer of poetry and prose

Mor Jokai (1824-1904), historical novelist, also poet and playwright

Attila Jozsef (1905-37), poet

Janos Kadar (1912-89), first secretary of Communist Central Committee

Mihaly Karolyi (1875-1955), first prime minister of Hungary (1918-19)

Zoltan Kocsis (1952-   ), pianist and professor

Zoltan Kodaly (1882-1967), composer; collector of and writer on Hungarian folk music

Lajos Kossuth (1802-94), patriot and statesman; headed movement for independence

Bela Kun (1885-1937), Hungarian Jewish Communist; organized Communist revolution in Budapest in 1919

Franz Lehar (1870-1948), composer of operettas, including *The Merry Widow*

Franz Liszt, (1811-86), piano virtuoso and composer

Imre Madach (1823-64), poet and playwright

Viktor Madarasz (1830-1907), painter

Matthias Corvinus (1443-90), king of Hungary (1458-90)

Kalman Mikszath (1847-1910), novelist and political journalist

Ferenc Molnar (1878-1952), playwright, novelist, and short-story writer

Laszlo Nemeth (1901-1975), essayist, social and historical dramatist

Sandor Petofi (1823-49), called Hungary's national poet

Prince Ferenc Rakoczi (1676-1735), led rebellion against Austria (1703); prince of Transylvania (1704-11), defeated by Austrians in 1711

Erno Rubik (1910-   ), aircraft designer and designer of Rubik's Cube

St. Stephen (977-1038), first king of Arpad Dynasty, called "the Apostle of Hungary"

Sigismund (1368-1437), king of Hungary (1387-1437)

Georg Solti (1913-   ), Hungarian-born former conductor of the Chicago Symphony Orchestra

Karoly Szakonyi (1931-   ), playwright

Istvan Szechenyi (1791-1860), soldier and statesman; founded Hungarian National Academy of Sciences (1825)

Bertalan Szekely (1835-1910), painter

Albert Szent-Gyorgyi (1893-1986), scientist and professor, received Nobel Prize for medicine in 1937

Sandor Szokolay (1931-   ), contemporary composer

Aron Tamasi (1897-1966), novelist

Mihaly Vorosmarty (1800-55), poet and dramatist

INDEX

Page numbers that appear in boldface type indicate illustrations

About the Author

   Martin Hintz, a former newspaper reporter, has written more than a dozen books for young people. The subjects range from training elephants to other social studies titles included in the Childrens Press Enchantment of the World series. He and his family currently live in Milwaukee, Wisconsin. Hintz has a master's degree in journalism and is a professional travel writer/photographer who has won numerous awards for his work.

   For help in the research of Enchantment of the World: Hungary, the author wishes to thank the Hungarian National Tourist Office; the Information Office of the Council of Ministers, Hungarian People's Republic; Tourinform; Pal and Ilonka Konyves-Toth; Istvan Megyes; Zoltan Hacker; Magda Volgyesi; Rita Vargas; Gyula Lazay; Bertalouise Pager, Ibolya Lorincz, and the pupils of the Josef Egry School in Budapest; Sefan Fuszenecker; Christina Sauter; Eva Miho; Kathrin Ladanyi; Janos Molnar; Sandor Branstetter; Peter Bengyel; Zoltan Kody; George Tabori; Sebestyen Tibot; Eva Tuschak, and IBUSZ: Janna Mathiasz; journalists Attila Bekes, Zsolt Szebeni, Gyorgy Szaraz, and Zsolt Szaboky; Maria Visontay; Miklos Kapolnasi; Sandor Lakatos; Dr. Dezso Szilagyi, and the Hungarian State Puppet Theater; and Ilonka Fischer.